An Historical Account

of

CHARLES ISLAND

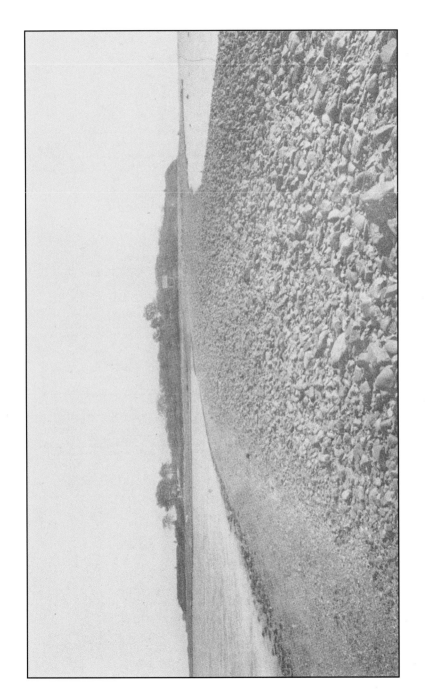

Sandbar Leading to Charles Island
Author's Collection

An Historical Account

of

CHARLES ISLAND

Milford, Connecticut

MICHAEL C. DOOLING

THE CARROLLTON PRESS

MMVI

First Edition

ISBN # 0-9627424-1-4

Printed in the United States of America by InstantPublisher.com

Contents

Introduction

As City Historian I receive many questions on a wide variety of topics. A few I can answer readily, but for most I have to rely on sources beyond myself. I have learned over time there are certain individuals to whom I can refer questioners on a particular topic. There are also printed sources I have learned to consult.

Probably the most popular topic among questioners is Charles Island, which seems to inspire a great fascination, perhaps because of its relative inaccessibility, perhaps because of its varied past. People want to know about the Dominican Retreat, the hotel, the prize fight, the fertilizer factory and, most of all, the legend of Captain Kidd and his treasure.

This little book has been impressively and thoroughly researched and will be of great help to me in doing my job as "answer man." There is much in it I had not known about the island and I found it to be interesting reading. It is hard to imagine there is anything about the place that Michael Dooling could have missed.

Richard N. Platt, Jr.
Milford City Historian
4 July 2006

Foreword

Charles Island has fascinated Milford residents and visitors to the area for many generations. Legends of Captain Kidd's treasure, hearsay of a once thriving resort, and the remnants of a religious retreat house imbue them with dreams of riches and curiosity about the past. Like the sparse and storm-shattered remains of the structures that once graced the island, only bits and pieces of its history survive. Reliable information regarding Charles Island is strewn about here and there, and the historical landscape is littered with misinformation, speculations and fictions.

In this work, I have re-constructed the island's history from a wide variety of sources including maps from the 17th to 19th centuries, town records, newspaper accounts & advertisements, 19th century journals, personal recollections from visitors to the resort that thrived there, photographs from its days as a religious retreat, etc. Combined they offer a unique view of the island and a perspective that until now has been lost with time.

I want to express my appreciation to the following individuals and institutions for their generous assistance: Bridgeport Public Library, Connecticut Department of Environmental Protection – Wildlife Division, The Connecticut Historical Society Museum, Connecticut State Library, Fairfield Historical Society, Mr. Paul Fusco, Library of Congress, Rebecca Slaughter and the Mattatuck Museum, Middlebury Public Library, Mr. Richard Platt - Milford Municipal Historian, Milford Historical Society, the staff and resources of the Genealogy Room of the Milford Public Library, Mr. Alan Jepson and the Milford City Clerk's Office, Mystic Seaport Museum, National Archives of The Netherlands, New Haven Colony Historical Society, the New Netherland Institute, the Dominican Archives at Providence College, St. Mary's Parish in New Haven, Silver Sands State Park, University of Connecticut Library, Dr. Christopher Parker, Mr. Edward Quick, Mrs. Jeanette W. Acton and the Walnut Beach - Myrtle Beach Historical Association, and the Yale University Libraries.

Courtesy of the Yale University Library

"Charles Island sits upon the flashing expanse of the Sound like an unreal thing of beauty, well covered with trees, a jewel set in the ever-changing sea, a landmark for skippers, a picture for artists."

William Howe Downes, 1889

Owners of Charles Island
1640 to Present

Year of Purchase	Names of Owners
1640	George Hubbard, Freeplanter (Milford)
Uncertain	Richard Bryan (Milford)
1657	Charles Deal (Milford)
c. 1685	Samuell & Pitty (Deal) Couch (Milford)
c. 1698	Elizabeth Couch (England)
Uncertain	Nathaniel Eels (Milford)
1711	Samuel Eels (Milford)
1742	Edward Allen (Milford later Southbury, CT)
1791	Samuel William Johnson (Stratford, CT)
1822	David Merwin & Samuel Burns (Milford)
1828	Samuel Burns (Milford)
1835	John Harris (New York City)
1841	George H. Paddock & Joseph Blunt (New York)
1845	William P. van Rensselaer (Rye, NY)
1852	Elizur E. Prichard (Waterbury, CT)
1862	Sarah J. Prichard (Waterbury, CT)
1888	Elizabeth F. Noble (Brooklyn, NY)
1902	George L. Lilley (Waterbury, CT)
1903	George J. Roberts (Philadelphia, PA)
1904	Connecticut Railway & Lighting Company
1927	Thomas F. Reilly (New Haven, CT)
1930	Dominican Fathers of the Province of St. Joseph
1941	Walter A. Peck (Westport, CT)
1943	First National Bank & Trust Company (Bridgeport)
1949	United Illuminating Company
1981 - Present	State of Connecticut

Compass Rose from Adriaen Block's Map, 1614
Nationaal Archief, The Netherlands, 4.VEL 520

European Discovery

Located in Long Island Sound about three-quarters of a mile from the settlement at Milford lies the little island known as Charles Island. One can reach it by boat or from the mainland by foot at low tide when a sandbar is gradually revealed. Technically speaking, the sandbar is a "tombolo," a sand or gravel bar that connects an island to the mainland or to another island. Only some fourteen acres large, Charles Island has a surprisingly rich history. In its pre-colonial days, it was a favorite haunt of the native inhabitants who called it Poquahaug. An abundance of clams could be found near the water's edge and along the rocky access to the island. So splendid was the island that Ansantawae, sachem of the Paugussett Tribe, is said to have spent his summers there.

The European discovery of Poquahaug can be traced back to the first Dutch explorers to sail through the Great Bay (Long Island Sound) and who mapped its coastlines. In November 1613, a group of Dutch fur traders from the van Tweenhuysen syndicate had been plying the waters of the Hudson River in two ships - the *Fortuyn* mastered by Hendrick Christiaensen and the *Tijger* commanded by Adriaen Block. The ships, fully loaded with furs, were preparing to sail back to Holland when the *Tijger* caught fire and was totally destroyed.

With winter approaching, the two crews put up shelters on Manhattan Island and proceeded to build a new ship. They spent the winter building the vessel and by spring had completed the 16-ton *Onrust* (meaning "restless") measuring only 44½ feet in length. The *Onrust* has the notable distinction of being the first ship built in the New World. The unfortunate fire that altered their plans to return home gave these fur traders time to explore the geography surrounding Manhattan. When they departed, instead of sailing out of the harbor into open water, they sailed northeast into unexplored waters.

No original logbooks or journals are known to exist from the 1614 voyage but as Block explored the area he recorded his observations on a map. His hand-drawn map survives today and is a reasonably accurate representation of the coastlines of what would become Connecticut and

Long Island. Fortunately for historians, a few years later another member of the Dutch West India Company, Johan de Laet, wrote a narrative of that historic voyage seemingly based on Block's original records.

The *Onrust* and its crew sailed into the Great Bay and passed a number of small islands, off what is now Norwalk. Captain Block named this cluster "Archipelagus" (spelled using the more familiar "Archipelagos" in some translations). Block's map clearly shows a dozen islands in the lower Sound along the Connecticut coast. The term "Archipelagus" and the islands appear in this vicinity on Dutch maps later in the 17th century and appear to be based on Block's voyage. In Laet's account of the voyage, no mention is made of Poquahaug specifically. However, he did describe New Haven harbor and the Quinnipiac River, which he named the "River of Royenberch," and mentions an island to the west of it:

> Four leagues[1] further to the west there lies a small island, where good water is to be found; and four leagues beyond there are a number of islands, so that Captain Adriaen Block gave the name Archipelagus to the group.[2]

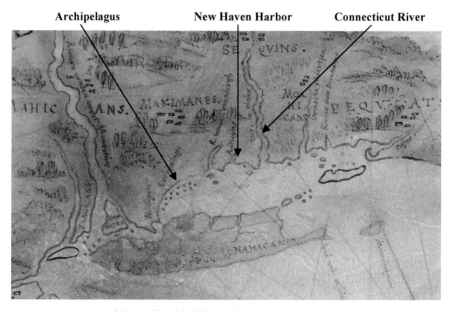

Adriaen Block's Map of the Great Bay, 1614
Nationaal Archief, The Netherlands, 4.VEL 520

There is confusion in the historical literature as to what island Laet was referring. One translation from the Dutch[3] stated, "Twelve miles further to the <u>east</u> (from the River of Royenberch) there lies a small island where good water is to be found…," which led at least one author to conclude the island was Falkner's Island off Guilford.[4] But the next part of the sentence reads, "and twelve miles <u>beyond</u> there are a number of islands, so that Captain Block gave the name 'Archipelagos' to the group." It is generally accepted the Archipelagos he referred to are the islands off Norwalk. The sentence in its entirety indicates the island to which he was referring was between New Haven and the Archipelagos – to the <u>west</u>. The translations from the later Latin and French editions[5] of Laet's account read, "Twelve miles <u>west</u> (of the River of Royenberch) an island presents itself, and soon after many more are seen, whence our people called this place Archipelago."

Given his approximate distances, the conversion of "leagues" into nautical miles (which wasn't standardized in the 17th century), inaccuracies in measurement, and not knowing his precise beginning and end-points it is difficult to determine exactly where he was referring. However, looking at Block's map the island Laet referred to would be about half way between New Haven harbor and the Norwalk islands. Although Johan de Laet only wrote of one island there (notable for its good water) Block's map clearly shows two islands – roughly between Milford and Bridgeport and one of them is very likely Charles Island.

There has been some speculation that Stratford Shoal (site of Stratford Shoal Light) was a more prominent above-water feature 400 years ago and that Block may have delineated it on his map. This dangerous reef is about three-quarters of a mile in length. By the early 19th century there was little of it visible and efforts to warn sailors to its dangers started about 1820. Whether it was prominent enough to be noted by Block two hundred years earlier is a matter of debate.

Another possibility is the now rocky Penfield Reef, home of the Penfield Reef Light further into the waters of Long Island Sound. Although mostly covered by water now, Penfield Reef was a more prominent island 400 years ago and cows were allowed to graze there by local farmers. Like Charles Island, Penfield Reef was connected to the mainland by a strip of land that is barely visible today. It is not known whether Charles Island, Stratford Shoal or then peninsular Penfield Reef had a good fresh water source in 1614.

On his map, Block penned a somewhat cryptic notation between the two islands and New Haven harbor. Barely visible and written at the intersection of two compass lines he wrote the words "De Keer." Block made many notations on his map including names of ships and individuals who were trading in various areas, names of islands, Indian tribes, etc. There are several definitions for "De Keer" – "time," "turning point," "course," "direction of movement," "opening," and many others. It isn't clear exactly what Block meant when he wrote those words nor is it clear if he was referring to the islands themselves or making some navigational notation. Other mapmakers copied his words on maps of the area until later in the 17th century.

Adriaen Block went on to explore the Connecticut River past Hartford and continued beyond the Great Bay to explore the area around Cape Cod. He was the first to discover that Long Island was, in fact, an island and he appears to be the first European to assign a name to it. In addition, it was his map that first properly portrayed a somewhat distorted representation of Manhattan as being surrounded by water. However, he is best remembered by the island that carries his namesake, Block Island. Although it was discovered and named Luisa Island by Giovanni da Verrazano in 1524, a shortened version of the name assigned by the Dutch - "Adriaen Block's Eylant" - is the one that remains to this day.

Upon his return home in October 1614, Block presented his report and map to the Amsterdam Trading Company, which turned the map over to the States General of Holland when it applied for a trading monopoly for the region between Philadelphia and Maine. The monopoly was granted for a three year period and that region became known as New Netherland.

Long Island Sound, 1685
Library of Congress

The Dutch weren't the only Europeans in the area in the early 17th century. In 1639, a company of forty English settlers purchased a large tract of land from the Paugussett tribe and named the new purchase Milford. The land purchase, completed in February of that year, "comprehended the tract of land lying between the East river and the Housatonnuc, and the sea with the island south, and the two mile Indian path to Paugusset (Derby) north."[6] The cost of the entire land purchase including the island Poquahaug was "6 coats, 10 blankets, 1 kettle, 12 hatchets, 12 hoes, 2 dozen knives, and a dozen small glasses (mirrors)."[7]

The following year the island was allotted to George Hubbard, a free planter who had transplanted himself from Wethersfield, and he later sold the property to Richard Bryan. On March 17, 1657 what had become known as Milford Island became the property of Charles Deal, who bought it with the intent of raising tobacco. The town of Milford granted him permission to purchase the island for the purpose of planting tobacco on the condition that the buildings he constructed were solely used for that purpose and that he should "not trade with the Dutch or Indians, nor suffer any

15

disorderly resort of seaman or others there."[8] It is from Charles Deal's ownership that the island receives its modern name. His attempt at planting was noteworthy only in that it was one of the earliest attempts at raising tobacco in colonial Connecticut. The little Milford plantation soon failed as the soil wasn't suitable for a tobacco crop.

Charles Deal died in 1685 and left the island with other property to his wife Pitty. After his death she married Samuell Couch, a "cloathmaker," and she died sometime thereafter. When Samuell died about 1698, he left a will that disposed of "my land lying in ye harbour of Milford aforementioned, commonly known as Milford Island or Charles Island."[9] He gave the land to his daughter Elizabeth, who lived in England, on the condition that she take personal possession within seven years after his death. If she did not take possession the island would be given to Nathaniel Eels.

Nathaniel purchased the lands from Elizabeth for a "valuable consideration" after which he sold the land to his brother Major Samuel Eels. In 1711, Samuel Eels petitioned the colony of Connecticut to grant him clear title to the land should an unknown heir of Charles Deal or Pitty appear or should the state decide that it had rights to the property. The state granted him unquestionable title to the land in May of that year - "Upon consideration whereof, this Assembly do accordingly give and grant, unto the said Samuel Eels, his heirs and assigns, all the right of this Colony whatsoever to the said lands, that hath accrued, or may accrue to them by the said law."[10]

By his petition to the state for clarification of property rights, it is uncertain if Samuel Eels was simply being careful about protecting his investment or if he suspected the property might hold something even more valuable worthy of legal protection. Just a few years earlier, during its ownership by the remote owner Elizabeth Couch, Charles Island earned its place in pirate lore. Three centuries later, people are still speculating whether the island that Samuel Eels purchased and so carefully protected was used by a reputed pirate to deposit part of his riches.

The Captain Kidd Legend

Legends of treasure buried along the shores of Long Island Sound have persisted for over three hundred years. Most of the stories have a common theme and a singular source - the missing treasure of one of the world's best-known pirates, Captain William Kidd. Unlike many such stories of hidden wealth, the legendary Kidd treasure is rooted in several compelling historical facts.

Piracy on the high seas, particularly in the Indian Ocean, was a pressing problem and the English monarchy decided to do something about it. Dealing with the problem fell into the hands of Richard Coote, Earl of Bellomont, the colonial governor of New England and New York. One of his main charges from the King was to suppress the piracy originating in the colonies. At the suggestion of one prominent colonist, Robert Livingston, William Kidd was recommended as the best man who could help accomplish the task. Kidd was a respected sea captain residing in New York with his wealthy wife Sarah and their daughter.

Captain William Kidd was born c. 1645 in Scotland and at an early age went to sea as a merchant seaman. He earned the reputation on both sides of the Atlantic of being a bold and skilled adventurer. In 1696, he was granted a commission to apprehend pirates by the King of England through Lord Bellomont. Kidd was legally a privateer with the authority to seize ships and cargos of pirates and ships sailing under the flags of enemies of the throne. "Goods, Merchandizes, Treasure and other things which shall be taken from said Pirates"[11] was to be divided by Bellomont, Kidd, Livingston and several others. A 275-ton vessel named the *Adventure Galley* was fitted out in London with thirty-two cannon. In July 1696, Kidd sailed her into New York harbor and began to recruit a crew of 150 men to help him with his new enterprise. Sprinkled among them were a number of men who were known pirates.

The agreement allowed Kidd to cruise against the pirates "who prowled between the Cape of Good Hope and the Straights of Malacca"[12] and also permitted him to capture ships belonging to France since she was an enemy of the British government. In January 1697 the *Adventure Galley* arrived off the coast of Madagascar, a haven for pirates, to search for prizes but didn't find any. As a matter of fact, nearly a year passed before Kidd encountered any pirates or French-flagged vessels. This resulted in most of the crew wanting to turn the *Adventure Galley* into a pirate ship, taking ships and cargos regardless of the flag being flown. Rumors abounded that Kidd himself had turned to piracy, while he had actually tried to keep his crew in line. At one point, Kidd had an argument with a member of his crew, William Moore, who wanted to capture a Dutch vessel outside the bounds of Kidd's commission. In a fit of anger, Kidd struck the would-be pirate in the head with a heavy wooden bucket. The man later died from a fractured skull.

In February 1698, Captain Kidd spotted the *Quedah Merchant* off the Malabar coast. She was riding low in the water from her magnificent cargo of silk, opium, jewels, silver and gold. There was some question over the legality of taking her as a prize. The merchants on board were Armenian, the Captain was English, the English East India Company had a financial interest in the cargo and the ship carried a French flag but was owned by an Indian. When the ship's papers were presented to Kidd, they were clearly French. He took the vessel and all her cargo and returned to Madagascar, where most of his unhappy crew mutinied and joined the ranks of pirate Robert Culliford. There Kidd scuttled the *Adventure Galley* and sailed toward America in the *Quedah Merchant* carrying his gold, silver and jewels. When he arrived in the Caribbean in April the following year he was informed that he and his crew were condemned pirates and orders had been given to seize him on sight. In order to help avoid capture, Kidd purchased a 55-ton sloop, the *St. Antonio*. He headed north and hoped to clear his name and prove he had seized a French vessel by presenting the ship's papers from the *Quedah Merchant*.

Captain Kidd left the Caribbean on May 15th, sailed toward New England and into Long Island Sound with about forty men and stopped at Oyster Bay on June 9, 1699. There he took on board his lawyer, James Emott, and proceeded to Block Island. Remaining in that safe haven, Kidd sent Emott to Boston to consult with Lord Bellomont as to how he might obtain safe passage there so he could exonerate himself from the piracy charges. Emott also turned over to Bellomont the French passes from the *Quedah Merchant* as proof of Kidd's innocence.

Safe passage was promised by Bellomont and the ship arrived in Boston on July 1, 1699, nearly empty. Kidd was arrested six days after his arrival and the following April arrived in England to be tried for the murder of William Moore and for piracy. Kidd claimed that a near mutinous crew forced him to piracy, but pleaded to no avail. The French papers from the *Quedagh Merchant*, that would likely have cleared him, somehow disappeared and were not presented as evidence during the trial. Kidd was convicted on both counts and was hanged at London's Execution Dock on May 23rd, 1701. In a last ditch effort for clemency, a few days before he was executed, Kidd wrote a letter to the Speaker of the House and in effect started a worldwide hunt for his fortune: [13]

> *Sir,*
> *The sence of my present Condition (being under*
> *Condemnation) - and the thoughts of haveing been imposed*
> *on by such as seek't my destruction therby to fulfill their*
> *ambitious desieres - makes me uncapable of Expressing my*
> *selfe in those terms as I ought. Therefore I doe most humbly*
> *pray that you will be pleased to represent to the Hon'bl.*
> *House of Commons that in my late proceedings in the*
> *Indies I have lodged goods and Tresure to the value of one*
> *hundred thousand pounds which I desiere the Government*
> *may have the benefitt of. In order thereto I shall desiere no*
> *manner of liberty but to be kept prisonner on board such*
> *shipp as may be appointed for that purpose, and only give*
> *the necessary directions, and in case I faile therin I desire*
> *no favour but to be forthwith Executed acording to my*
> *Sentence...*

> *S'r Y'r Unfortunate humble servant*

> *Wm Kidd*

Kidd was survived by his wife and child in New York and by dozens of legends regarding the whereabouts of his treasure trove. The origin of the local treasure stories relate to his voyage to Boston to defend himself. Kidd reputedly "set Goods on Shore at several Places"[14] and distributed most of his cargo and wealth from the *St. Antonio*.

Several locations are claimed to be repositories for Kidd's gold. Undoubtedly, the most well-known period in the history of Charles Island relates to the legendary treasure buried by Captain Kidd on that final voyage. Stories persist that Kidd off-loaded and buried part of his treasure on the island. Over the centuries, many people have dug around the island in attempts to find the treasure. One bit of local folklore,[15] first published in 1838, relates the story of one such attempt:

> It being said that the notorious Kidd buried money on the south side of it (Charles Island), beside a rock, two or three persons went privately, on a moon light night, to dig for it. After much preparatory ceremony, such as drawing a circle round the rock, and reciting some words of incantation, they began to dig, and so far succeeded as to hit the lid of the iron box, when looking up into the air, they saw coming down direct upon them "the figure of a man without a head." They dropped their spades, and run as most others would have done, and escaped. Looking toward the spot they saw it enveloped in smoke and blue flame. Returning to the island the next day, their spades had disappeared, they found the ground smooth, and no traces left of its having been dug.

Although the headless man story is dubious in detail, there is evidence that Kidd not only anchored in Long Island Sound in June of 1699 but that he visited Milford, socializing, imbibing and carousing with some of the local residents. He reputedly came to Milford two to three times and walked openly in the town. A faded and torn letter[16] written by a young woman and dated 1699 was discovered in a bundle of papers in the garret of one of Milford's oldest houses and described one of his visits:

...Aunt Prudence has told you of ye visit from Capt. Kidd,
from ye craft wh. was seen to come in ye harbour at 7 of ye
clock in ye evening. He stayed in ye house till in ye early
morning, and sat all ye night by ye fire with Jacobeth and
Thomas Welsh[17] carrying himself in an uncivil and bold
manner. I told Aunt Prudence yt he will come to trouble in
ye sinful way, wh. he has done, - for Zachariah Whitman[18]
has told us all about him. I asked Jacobeth ye next day if yt
Robert (sic) Kidd[19] was to come in ye town of Milford any
more - for noe one will have him in this plantation. I want
to tell you, cousin Thankful,[20] what he did: when he came in
ye room he put his arms about my waiste, and kyssed me,
wh made Jacobeth laugh and Thomas Welsh cough.
Jacobeth says yt Capt. Bob (sic) is not so bad as ye folks
say, and yt he was a little wild. But Aunt Prudence will not
hear any good word spoken of him whatsoever, and has
told Thomas Welsh what she heard about him. I overheard
Jacobeth say yt Kidd was going on a long cruise, and yt he
had left some things with him. I am going to tell Aunt
Prudence all about it, and find out what they are.

Your cousin,

Patience Tuttle

Whether Kidd left treasure with Jacobeth on the mainland at Milford or simply gifted him a part of his ship's less valuable cargo, it may never be known. And, whether he buried part of his plunder on Charles Island during his visit that year is still a matter of much speculation. The first printed appearance of this letter appears to be in *The New England Magazine* in 1889. In the article, there was no indication as to where or when the letter was found or who possessed it at the time of its publication.

Legends of Kidd having buried his treasure exist along the shoreline of Connecticut include Welch's Point[21] (on the Milford shore, east of Charles Island) where Kidd supposedly buried the treasure next to a rock. And not far away, according to local fable, a slave was lying on Stratford Point (a short distance to the west of Charles Island) on a moonlit night when he observed a large boat come ashore. A group of men dug a hole in the sand and buried a large chest. When they discovered they were being watched they chased the slave but failed to catch him. The men allegedly unearthed the chest and buried it farther to the west. With this story as their guideline, a group of men from Bridgeport banded together in the 1850s and attempted to find the rumored treasure. They plowed large stretches of the beach in what became known as "The Gold Diggings" but like other such attempts, had no luck.

Near the town of Branford, a few miles east of New Haven, lay the Thimble Islands where stories of Kidd's treasure abound on at least three of the islands. A pirate ship is said to have sought shelter in High Island's harbor and the curious locals who sailed out to greet it were lucky to have made it back alive. The story was firmly entrenched by the beginning of the nineteenth century and the obligatory speculation of buried treasure was propounded by the resort hotels on the islands to encourage the tourist trade. One such hotel on Pot Island sported Captain and Mrs. Kidd's initials "supposed to have been inscribed by his own hand" on a rock near the hotel. Nearby Money Island lays claim to "Kidd's Cave" with a reputed underwater entrance. Little in the way of physical evidence support the speculation of Kidd's gold in the Thimbles, except in 1924 a New Haven fireman found a gold ring believed to have been crafted in the East Indies.[22]

Most of the region's tales of Kidd's buried treasure emanate from the historically factual story of William Kidd having buried part of his riches on Gardiner's Island at the outer reaches of Long Island. On some early maps Gardiner's is misspelled "Garner's" and on others it is referred to as the "Isle of Wight." On his way to Boston in 1699, Kidd lay at anchor off Long Island for several days. In an attempt to protect his wealth, he buried chests containing gold, silver and jewels on Gardiner's island. He left other goods in the possession of the island's owner, John Gardiner, and with some old friends including Captain Thomas Paine of Rhode Island. Kidd also gave a significant cache to Captain Thomas Clark for safekeeping. Clark reputedly stored it in a warehouse in Stamford and is believed to have turned it over (or at least part of it) to authorities after Kidd's arrest.

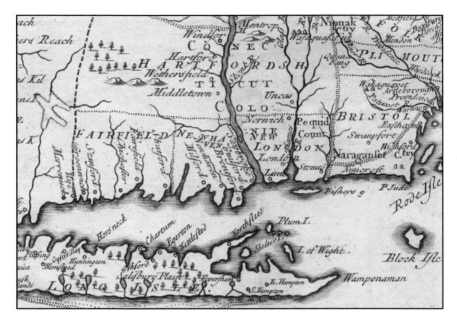

Map Showing Gardiner's Island (I. of Wight), 1720
Author's Collection

After Kidd was arrested in Boston authorities learned he had deposited a quantity of his wealth on Gardiner's Island. Lord Bellomont despatched three commissioners to the island to retrieve the gold, silver and jewels buried there. To this day, a simple granite marker rests on Gardiner's Island that reads, "Capt. Kidd's treasure was buried in this hollow and recovered 1699."

When inventoried, the total amount was staggering;[23] the value of Kidd's treasure found on Gardiner's Island was about £14,000. As large as the cache was, it was considerably less that the £100,000 William Kidd claimed to have hidden in various places. It is uncertain and will always be a matter of speculation whether Kidd exaggerated the amount in an attempt to save himself or had actually buried his treasure trove. The only area known with certainty to have been used by Kidd to leave valuables with others or to bury his treasure is the area around Long Island Sound and Block Island Sound. There is no existing evidence anywhere else.

Inventory of the Cache on Gardiner's Island

		Ounces
1.	One bag of dust-gold	$60^{3/4}$
2.	One bag of coyned gold	11
	and in it silver	124
3.	One bag of dust-gold	$24^{3/4}$
4.	One bag silver rings & precious stones	$17^{3/8}$
5.	One bag silver buttons and a lamp	29
6.	One bag broken silver	$173^{1/2}$
7.	One bag of gold bars	$353^{1/4}$
8.	One bag of gold bars	$238^{1/2}$
9.	One bag of dust-gold	$59^{1/2}$
10.	One bag of silver bars	212
11.	One bag of silver bars	309

Whether pirate or privateer, Kidd left us with one of the world's great legends of buried treasure. So permeating is the historical account of Captain Kidd and so convinced are the treasure seekers that more gold, silver and precious gems exist that the "remaining" treasure continues to be sought. Despite the passage of more than 300 years, the Kidd legend is alive and well.

As recently as 1992, an expedition, headed by professional treasure hunter Don Johnson, surveyed Charles Island in search of the treasure. His team identified a group of burial spots, arranged in a triangle and resting between eighteen and thirty feet below the surface. With the aid of electronic equipment, including ground penetrating radar, he determined the objects each measured 9" x 12", weighed forty pounds each, and were comprised of gold and copper.[24] Attempts by the treasure hunter to excavate on the island became bogged down with concerns by the State Department of Environmental Protection and no excavation by the Johnson expedition was conducted. The discovery of an ancient gold coin or silver ring anywhere in the vicinity of Long Island Sound will keep the legends alive for several more centuries.

Howard Pyle's Depiction of Kidd on Gardiner's Island

Harper's New Monthly Magazine, 1894

From Farmland to Summer Residence

Charles Island had several owners during the 18th century and early 19th century and little of historical note has been uncovered for that period. The advent of the American Revolution focused the Milford townspeople on defense. In May 1775 the town voted "that the Great Guns be mounted and made ready for use, and the selectmen provide powder and balls at the town's expense."[25] The following February an ordinance was passed to conserve gunpowder, "that no person or persons whatsoever, shall, by sporting or fowling, fire away any of that necessary article, within the limits of the town, upon penalty of 1£. lawful money for each offence.[26] A few months later, a fortified gun battery consisting of six cannon and a twenty-man garrison, was put in place on the point at the west side of the harbor and named Fort Trumbull. A company of minute-men was organized and several Milford men joined Washington's army.

Milford's defenders apparently saw no action even when four British ships anchored off the Milford coast in 1777 within sight of Charles Island. The inhabitants expected an attack and the entire town was on alert but the only assault was on the Miles Merwin homestead on Pond Point. A small group of British soldiers made landfall and pillaged the house but left the structure intact. Other than that incident, the town of Milford saw no military action and didn't suffer any real damage during the Revolution.

Some authors have speculated that Charles Island may have played a role in the development of David Bushnell's submarine, called the *Turtle*. The *Turtle* was designed to carry explosives that could be attached to the hulls of British ships with the intent of sinking them while at anchor. Bushnell, a native of Saybrook and Yale graduate, likely built the vessel on Poverty Island in the Connecticut River and tested it in the waters of the Connecticut River and in Long Island Sound.

In August 1776, Bushnell brought the submarine to New York to attack the British man-of-war *Asia*. Bushnell's brother was to be the navigator but had become quite ill and the planned assault had to be halted. Ezra Lee, a sergeant from a Connecticut regiment, volunteered to step in and navigate the *Turtle* but needed to be trained in its operation. The speculation about

Charles Island probably originates from a letter written by Lee several years after the events in which he described his involvement; it reads in part:

> *...General Parsons sent for me & two others, who had given in our names to go in a fireship if wanted, to see if we would undertake the enterprise – we agreed to it...but first returned with the machine down Sound and on our way practised with it in several harbors. We returned as far back as Saybrook with Mr. Bushnell.*[27]

David Bushnell's *Turtle*
Courtesy of the Yale University Library

Lee made no mention of specific locales for the tests and any number of good locations could have been used. It is unlikely they would have tested the *Turtle* in harbors with much shipping activity as the project was secret and there were plenty of British sympathizers who might have reported what they saw. Quiet inlets and the Sound-side of islands that would have blocked the view from shore may well have been used by Bushnell to train the new navigator.

During the War of 1812, a minor incident occurred involving British warships. At midnight on October 1, 1814 three British vessels were spotted off the coast near Black Rock in Bridgeport and there were reports of heavy gun fire near New Haven. The local militia was called to action - "Ships ware at anchor about 8 miles out as they imedialy hove about and stod of when the alarrum guns ware fired." During the cover of night the ships moved off and information was received the next day that they had anchored "at Charles Isleand 4 miles east." The ships left the area with no further incident.[28]

Charles Island was undeveloped, except for farming activities, up to its purchase by a wealthy English gentleman from New York City. In 1835, Major John Harris, Esq. purchased the island for $800[29] and built a beautiful summer residence there. The big home, built on the highest ground, had verandas encircling it on the first and second stories. Harris elegantly furnished the house and spent $14,000 grading and landscaping the island making it resemble "a large green inverted saucer."[30]

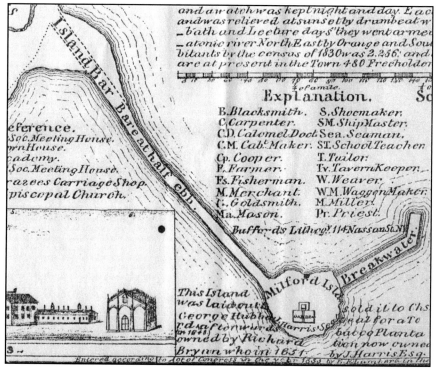

Map Showing John Harris' House and Garden, 1835
Author's Collection

There are scant records containing details of Harris' life; some say he was a wealthy New York merchant. A day book[31] listing daily business transactions from Adolphus Baldwin's general store on Broad Street near the corner of Wharf Lane in Milford finds Harris (or more likely a member of his domestic staff) to be a frequent customer. Every few days, items were charged to John Harris' account – mostly lard, eggs, cheese, smoked beef, pork, oil, matches, candles, oats, hay, powder and shot, and even two hymn books. During his ownership, Charles Island was sometimes referred to as "Major's Island," but the name couldn't compete with its historically entrenched name. Major Harris' health failed about the time he finished improving his island paradise.

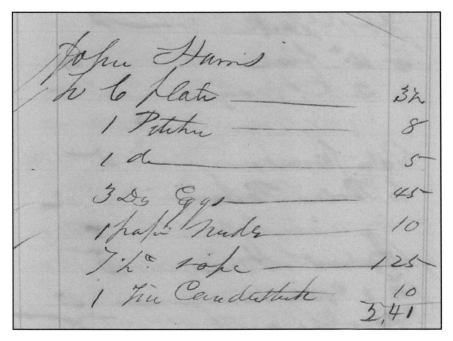

Entry in Adolphus Baldwin's Day Book, 1836
Manuscripts Collection, Connecticut State Library

The property was sold in 1841 and passed through the hands of George H. Paddock and Joseph Blunt before it was purchased by William Patterson van Rensselaer. Rensselaer was the son of Stephen and Cornelia van Rensselaer, a Yale graduate and was a major landholder near Albany. He lived on the family estate at Resselaerswyck until major problems arose in the area with renters.

The family property had been part of the leasehold system in which portions were rented to farmers who would work the land. The landowners not only received lease payments but also took a substantial percentage of the profits of the farmers. In 1839, after the death of William's father and as stated in his will, his heirs attempted to collect $300,000 in back rent. The farmers revolted and caused civil disruption and violence until the laws changed in 1846. For safety's sake, Rensselaer moved his family to Norwalk, Connecticut and later to Rye, New York. He also purchased the Charles Island property in 1845, probably as a summer retreat.

Rensselaer owned the island until April 1852 when he sold it to Elizur E. Prichard of Waterbury, Connecticut for $2,500 - one hundred dollars down with a $2,400 note due in four months. Prichard (spelled "Pritchard" in some sources) was a wealthy button manufacturer who had retired that year and used the house on Charles Island as his summer residence. According to one account, he spent $10,000 making the island "a combined park, lawn, orchard and garden."[32] Prichard's investment in the property was significant and he had plans for the island far beyond its use as a summer residence by him and his family.

Agreement between van Rensselaer and Elizur Prichard

Collection of Mattatuck Museum, Waterbury, CT

The Charles Island Resorts

With all his renovations completed, on June 22nd 1853 Elizur Prichard opened his spacious home to visitors as a summer resort and hotel he initially called "Island House." During the summer months, Prichard lived in the island mansion with his wife Betsey J. (Cooper) Prichard and their three daughters Elizabeth (who died a year after the resort opened), Katherine and Sarah. In the off-season they returned to their home in Waterbury. The Prichard family was one of the earliest to settle in Waterbury and had originally emigrated from Milford, possibly descending from after-planter Roger Pritchard who settled there in 1653.

Elizur E. Prichard
Collection of Mattatuck Museum
Waterbury, CT

Prichard's resort got off to a slow start. Difficulties crossing the sandbar from the mainland and lack of boat service to the island kept large numbers of people away. The problem was somewhat remedied in 1855 when steamboats from New Haven started taking visitors there for pleasure excursions twice a week during the summer months.[33] At this point in the resort's history, it was meant to be a quiet retreat for its guests. In way of amusements the resort offered bathing, boating, fishing and strolling about the grounds. A few years later, several other attractions would be added for the enjoyment of visitors to the island. Along the way, the name of the resort changed to "Charles Island House," evidenced by some of the resort's records kept by the owner. Word about the resort gradually spread and guests started to arrive from all points on the eastern seaboard.

31

Advertising Broadside, 1853
Collection of Mattatuck Museum, Waterbury, CT

Surprisingly, the Guest Register[34] for the Charles Island House from the summer of 1856 has survived the years. The hotel appears to have done a brisk business that summer with guests hailing from the Connecticut shoreline communities, Naugatuck Valley towns, as well as from New York, Massachusetts, New Jersey, Pennsylvania, Alabama and Georgia. Several sea captains frequented the hotel, some with their ladies. A guest named Elmer Palmley wrote in the register that he was from "Nowhere," a gentleman from Milford registered simply under the name "Dandy Jack," and a William F. Hall wrote in the register that he was "a missionary to the cannibals of Jersey – sixty-two miles from home and a stranger in a foreign land with nothing to eat."

Before the 1857 summer season, Prichard made extensive renovations to the place including the addition of a large room on the roof. He placed the resort under new management and re-opened the house to summer guests in 1857 naming it "Ansantawae House," after the Paugussett Indian Sachem who had made his mark on the deed for the land that became Milford in 1639. An advertising circular was sent to prospective visitors inviting them to the improved resort:

> *Dear Sir - Having taken the above delightful summer resort under our special supervision and management, we take this method to inform you or your friends who should feel disposed to visit the Sea=shore, that we feel confident in assuring you nothing will be wanting to make your stay agreeable and satisfactory. The Island is accessible by any of the accommodation trains on the New York, New Haven and Springfield Railroads, stopping at Milford, Conn.*

Respectfully yours, &c.,

Denslow & Adams

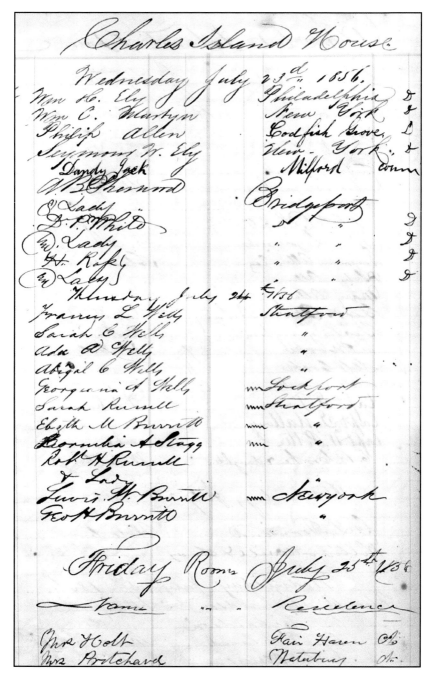

Guest Register for Charles Island House, 1856
Collection of Mattatuck Museum, Waterbury, CT

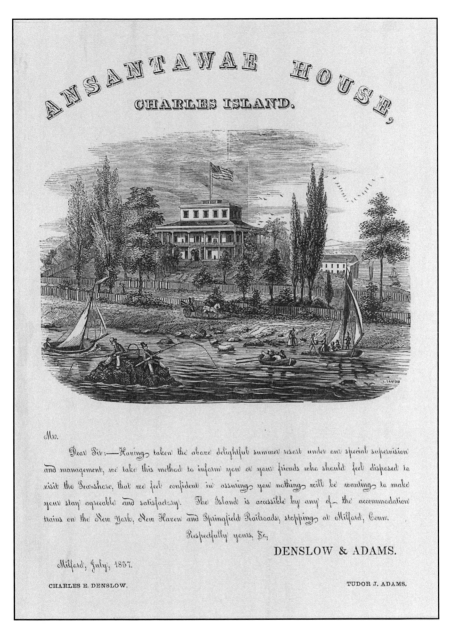

Advertising Circular, 1857

Upon its reopening, the resort was run by Charles E. Denslow and a Mr. Tudor J. Adams. Mr. Denslow's mother was responsible for the general management of the mansion. A year later, J. W. Burgess, formerly of the popular Allyn House Hotel in Hartford replaced Mr. Adams as one of the proprietors.[35] The resort offered Breakfast at 7:00, Dinner at 1:00 and Tea at 6:00, and the reviews were quite favorable.

One guest in 1857 complimented her stay there and wrote, "The table is excellent, and every thing about the establishment is the model of neatness and order. With commodious rooms opening from each story upon broad piazzas extending all round the house – grounds dotted with hundreds of shade-trees – and a sea-breeze from all quarters – visitors know nothing of the sultry heat that reigns in the town, the city, or the country. Ample provision is made for bathing, fishing, and other methods of diversifying the time…"[36]

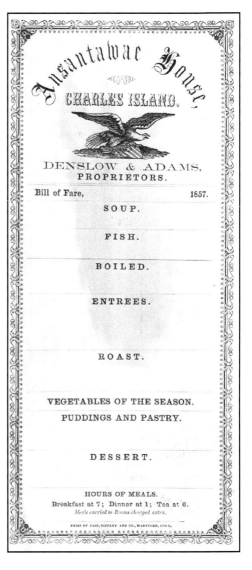

Bill of Fare, 1857

© The Connecticut Historical Society Museum, Hartford, Connecticut

NEW SUMMER RESORT.

ANSANTAWAE HOUSE,

CHARLES ISLAND.

 Is now opened for the reception of visitors. The house has been entirely renovated and fitted up in the most perfect order, and the proprietors intend making it the most popular house on Long Island Sound. It is believed that its beautiful location, the delightful scenery, and its advantages for fishing, bathing, boating, and the care which will be taken for the comfort and luxury of the guests, will make it the pleasantest watering place on this coast. It is easy of access; passengers can take any of the accommodation trains to Milford, and thence by Carriages or Boats, (at their option) to the House; it can be reached in two hours from Hartford.

Je 30   18d*   DENSLOW & ADAMS, Proprietors.

Newspaper Advertisement, 1857[37]

Another writer mocked the women who visited the Ansantawae House, encumbered with packages and extra band-boxes for their finery, by referring to them as "Flora M'Flimseys."[38] This term originated in a hugely popular poem, "Nothing to Wear," that had appeared in *Harper's Weekly* in early 1857.[39] It related the story of Flora M'Flimsey, a society belle who constantly shopped for new clothes yet never seemed to have anything to wear.

Visitors often took a train into Milford and then a horse-drawn carriage south to the vicinity of Burn's Point where the "Road to Charles Island" ran along the shore to the sandbar. From there, access to the island was attained by continuing via carriage, or by walking across the sandbar that connects the island to the mainland at low tide, or by taking a small boat. The Sharpie was one of the most popular crafts to use and they were plentiful on Long Island Sound. These long, narrow, flat-bottomed boats were rigged with two sails and were popular in the oystering trade and for transporting small numbers of people along the coast.

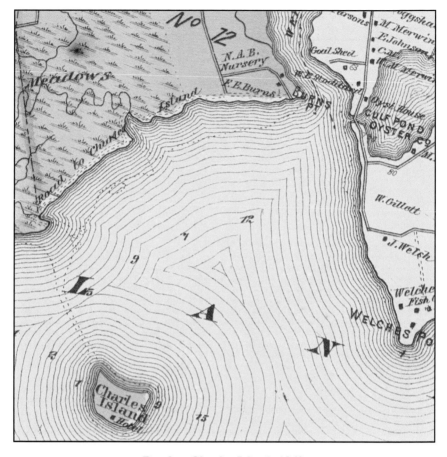

Road to Charles Island, 1868
Author's Collection

The newly renovated resort received the acclaim of its guests. In 1858, one satisfied visitor wrote[40]:

> ...At high tide, the island is reached in a beautiful little boat, of the form called a Sharpie. We found the sail across very delightful. The air was fresh, and the boat dashed gallantly over the waves and landed us at the foot of this little gem of the Sound. The island is circular in its shape, rising up in the centre to a height of fifty feet above low water mark. The top is crowned with the house which is buried in a forest of cherry trees of a large growth, and of

size sufficient to furnish all the shade needed around the house and around a lovely little flower garden well protected from the winds of the Sound. From the top of the house there is a very extensive view both up and down the Sound. In the evening, six light-houses can be counted from it...

...As a place of resort, Charles Island has many attractions...The bowling alley, the bar, and the rooms where young men can lodge, are at the bottom of the hill, so as not to disturb the quiet or invalids. It is an excellent place to which to take children and invalids. Families can have all the comforts they wish. It is an excellent place for the newly married to spend the honeymoon. There are many romantic walks, and quiet nooks for resting places, with nothing but the bright waves of the Sound in sight, spotted with the distant white sail. It is an excellent place for the betrothed to indulge in evening strolls with the bright moon kissing wavelets below them. The vows there registered the moon will never tell, nor the distant light-house reveal the kisses it may witness...We say to all who wish a few days relaxation at the seaside – Go to Charles Island.

The peaceful resort was not without its troubles. Late in July 1859, a fire destroyed the barn attached to the house. Elizur Prichard had gone into the barn carrying a candle a half hour before he discovered the fire. Although Prichard tried to extinguish the fire, the barn and its contents and Prichard's horse were destroyed. According to news accounts, Prichard "was injured by over-exertion during the fire, and was taken bleeding internally." [41] Dr. Beardsley of Milford attended him and expressed hope his condition would not prove serious. His injuries were not life-threatening and his exertions saved the hotel from being destroyed.

Prichard's days on the island were relatively few. He had gone to Charles Island on Wednesday, November 28th, 1860 and was returning to the mainland on Thanksgiving Day. He walked on the sandbar and had nearly reached the shore when two hunters heard him cry for help. He said he felt faint and they assisted him toward shore. While they were carrying him, he lost consciousness and died in their arms. It was speculated that either he suffered from heart disease or had collapsed from exhaustion, as the tide had begun to come in and the water was rapidly rising over the sandbar making the walk difficult. At age 55, he left this life and bequeathed the island to his daughter Sarah J. Prichard, an aspiring author. Elizur also left Sarah with a considerable mortgage.

In hopes of paying off the debt, Sarah Prichard leased the island to a group of investors to run a much-expanded summer resort. The name of the new effort reverted back to the "Charles Island House." In 1866, it was reported that a "new three story building has been erected this season, containing a well lighted and spacious dining hall, together with eligible rooms elegantly furnished, large and airy, and having all the modern improvements."[42]

The new building expanded the hotel to a total of seventy-five rooms. Other improvements included a swimming bath with plank bottom, an aquarium (claimed to be the largest in the country and headlining P. T. Barnum's trained seal "Ned"),[43] pavilions, wharves and a fountain supplied with water from Long Island Sound fed by steam pump. The new investors reportedly laid out $15,000 for these improvements.[44]

The Old Gents Band from New Haven was booked for the season to provide musical entertainment for the guests. George G. Lillie, formerly of the Merchants' Hotel in New Haven started working at the Charles Island House as a clerk.[45] The new superintendent of the resort was Alfred A. Upson, who was responsible for catering and had worked at the Savin Rock House, and the proprietor was Edwin Barnes. The venture proved so successful that daily steamboat service was started from New Haven's Steamboat Wharf and from Bridgeport, the price only 75 cents.

HOTELS.

Charles Island House,

SITUATED ON AN

ISLAND OF BEAUTY,

 IN LONG ISLAND SOUND
midway between New Haven and Bridgeport, &
about an equal distance from either city is the

Favorite Summer Resort of the Season

New buildings and elegantly furnished rooms, a splendid dining hall and good tables are among the conveniences of the place.

The novelties and attractions of the Island offer extraordinary inducements to pleasure seekers to visit it.

THE BEAUTIFUL FOUNTAIN

Is a source of pleasure, the magnificent

SWIMMING BATH

A source of comfort; while the splendid

AQUARIUM,

With its trained SEAL, SEA TURTLES, and fine specimens of the finny tribe, amuse and delight thousands of visitors.

The large new PROMENADE HALL is free of charge to visitors.

A Refreshment Room and Ice Cream Saloon are in close proximity.

THE NEW AND COMMODIOUS STEAMERS

Alice E. Preston and Ella,

Ply between Charles Island and the cities of New Haven and Bridgeport, thrice daily, affording ample facilities for reaching the island and departing from it.

BARNES & RICE, Proprietors.

A. A. Upson, Superintendent   jy 23 – 6d

Newspaper Advertisement, 1866[46]

1866.   Excursion Steamboats.   1866.

DAILY SEASHORE LINE

On and after Monday, June 18th, the splendid and commodious Steamboats ALICE E. PRESTON and ELLA will make Daily Excursion (Sundays excepted), during the season, to the following places, viz: CHARLES ISLAND, THIMBLE ISLANDS, BRANFORD POINT and BRIDGEPORT.

Leave New Haven from Steamboat Wharf, for Charles Island and Bridgeport, at 10:15 a.m., 3 o'clock p.m. and 8 o'clock p.m.; Branford Point and Thimble Islands at 11 o'clock a.m.

Returning, leave Bridgeport at 8 o'clock a.m., 2 o'clock p.m. and 8 o'clock p.m.; Charles Island 9:30 a.m., 5:30 p.m. and 10:30 p.m.; Thimble Island at 1 o'clock p.m. and Branford Point at 2 o'clock p.m.

FARES - From New Haven to Charles Island, 50c.; Bridgeport, 65c.; Branford Point, 40c.; Thimble Islands, 50 c. Return trips equal rates. Parties of fifty and upward accommodated at special rates on application at the office of LESTER & WEBB, 201 Chapel Street, New Haven.

ROUND TRIP TO CHARLES ISLAND ……….. 75 cts.
ROUND TRIP TO BRIDGEPORT . ………... $1.00.

☛ At New Haven the Horse railroad cars on Chapel Street run between the railway station and steamboat wharf every twelve minutes.   je 15 2md

Newspaper Advertisement, 1866[47]

Sidewheel Steamer *Ella* Underway

© Mystic Seaport Collection, Mystic, CT

The island resort was thriving; according to one source over 20,000 people visited Charles Island by the beginning of August in 1866 and the season wasn't over yet.[48] It is known that P. T. Barnum visited the resort at least once and a friend reminisced, "When, on one occasion that I remember, he took two or three hundred people from several towns in the State, and from New York, to Charles Island, a summer place midway between Bridgeport and New Haven, the hospitality was royal, and even the steamboat tickets were mysteriously provided for all."[49] The success of the Charles Island House resort was described in another publication:

> ...in the summer of 1866, a connection was formed with New Haven and Bridgeport by steamboats, running several times daily, when the House became at once one of the most popular in the country. Under able and energetic management, it ought to become a place of decidedly fashionable resort. The House will accommodate about one hundred guests. The usual contrivances for passing time pleasantly are found here as at other sea side houses, together with the largest aquarium in the country, and an artificial swimming bath filled from the ocean by a steam engine. A remarkable peculiarity of the Island is its exemption from the annoyance of mosquitoes, flies, insects and vermin generally. No spot at the North presents greater inducements for the introduction of the fashion common at the Virginia Springs and elsewhere, of private parties erecting their own dwellings in which they can unite privacy for the families with the enjoyments of a frequented watering place.[50]

Exactly how long the Charles Island House thrived is uncertain and the reasons why it closed are lost to history. The best evidence indicates, that in spite of the favorable reception by its guests, the resort closed by 1868. Less genteel activities replaced the fine fashions, afternoon teas and generous hospitality offered to the guests of the popular resort.

In 1896, Milford resident and civil engineer L. Edmund Toocker took it upon himself to reconstruct the layout of the resort as it appeared in 1861. He sketched a bird's eye view of the island and mapped the various buildings of the resort. It is unclear what methods he used to determine placement of the various structures but it is likely he used existing foundations and any remaining structures combined with recollections as his guide. His effort provides a detailed study of the positions of the various features of the Charles Island House resort.

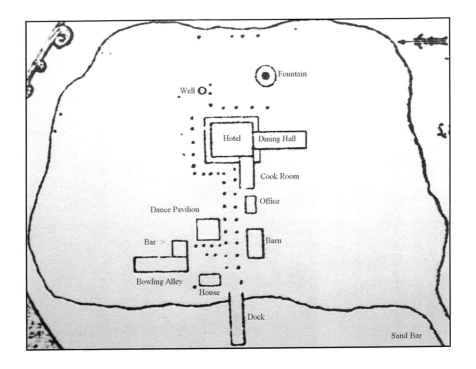

Detail from the L. Edmund Toocker Map
Courtesy of the Milford Public Library

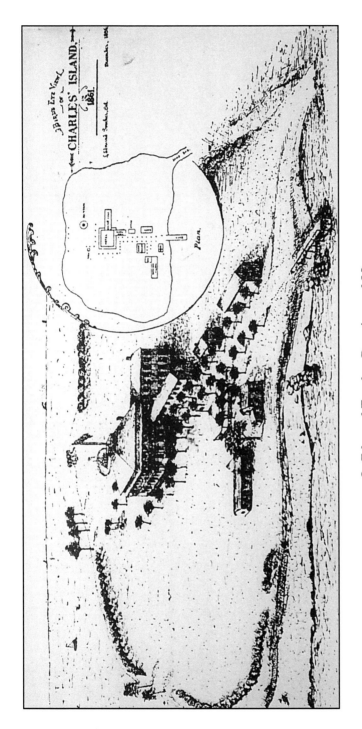

L. Edmund Toocker Drawing and Map

Courtesy of the Milford Public Library

The Famous Prize Fight

On April 12, 1870 Charles Island was to be used to stage a prize fight[51] between two contestants - Dan Kerrigan of Brooklyn, New York and Edward Touhey of New York City. En route to the match, Touhey met with near disaster. Early that morning, he hired a small "cock-shell" of a boat and an oarsman to take him to the island along with two other men who hoped to view the spectacle. Long Island Sound appeared calm when they left the shore but as they approached Charles Island, a NNE wind sprung up and started tossing the little craft. The water swelled and they started to take on water. About the time the situation looked hopeless, another boat was seen heading for a safe haven. The foursome hailed the boat and as it neared they swam to it and clambered aboard. The boat's owner, Dwight C. Lines, not only brought them to the safety of land but also saved them from another disaster that day.

While Touhey and his ill-fated party were warming themselves onshore, boxing fans of questionable character started to arrive in Milford from the area towns and "similar material arrived on the boat from New York." At nine o'clock in the morning Milford's first selectman contacted the sheriff informing him of the prize fight that was to take place and that "the village of Milford was filled with roughs, who were disturbing the good order and peace of the village, breaking into the stores and alarming the good people of that usually quiet town." He asked the sheriff to send officers to keep the peace.

Milford officials also requested help from New Haven police; New Haven's mayor and police chief immediately went to Milford to assess the situation. Meanwhile, Adjutant-General Merwin caught wind of the problem and ordered the militia to be ready for immediate service and included in his order the New Haven Grays, the Sarsfield Guard, the Foot Guard and the Montgomery Guard. One hundred and seventy-five soldiers and twenty-two policemen from New Haven arrived by train to restore order to the normally quiet community.

Militia Arriving at Charles Island
Courtesy of the Yale University Library

Back on Charles Island, when only Kerrigan showed up for the match the fight promoters declared him the winner by default. The audience was not happy and to pacify the increasingly unruly crowd they substituted two lesser weight boxers, a match made up at the last minute. Two fellows named Kelley and Williams pounded one another for three rounds and ended the match in a draw. The "admirers of the fistic art" started to leave the island about the same time the militia and police were arriving at the shore. Their only way off the island was to walk the sandbar that was nearly uncovered because of the receding tide. The island was described as a "man trap"[52] with the toughs' only exit blocked by the militia.

When some of the crowd starting to walk back to the mainland, the militia was ordered to "charge double quick" in order to reach the sandbar before the roughs got to shore. The soldiers reached the sandbar and the men from the boxing match saw them and retreated back to Charles Island. When the militia arrived on the island, the mob was ordered to the dancing pavilion and the island was searched. Two police officers turned over a boat on the shore and "discovered under it two bruisers, one of whom had his eye swelled shut, and the other who bore the most brutal looking 'mug' ever carried by one of the human species…" The novice boxers would have been far better off trying to row the boat off the island rather than hiding under it.

More than eighty men were marched off the island and through the town of Milford to the train that had brought the troops. The streets were lined with Milford citizens to watch the parade of rowdies. They were taken to New Haven and marched to the station-house and most spent the night in jail. There were four men who watched the entire unfolding of events from the safety of shore. No luckier men were in Milford that day than would-be prizefighter Edward Touhey and his three waterlogged companions.

This prize fight was not the last for Charles Island. In 1891, Bostonians Terry Lane and Dan Russell fought thirty-eight rounds with $500 for the winner.[53] The crowd was apparently more docile this time around and the militia wasn't called out to dish out another dose of "Puritan hospitality."[54]

Close of the Century

Charles Island was leased to the George W. Miles Company in 1868 to build a plant to produce fertilizer and fish oil. The Miles Company had been located on Pond Point about two miles east of Charles Island. In fact, it was one of two such plants in Milford – the other on Welch's Point. This type of malodorous manufacturing activity is inconsistent with a summer resort so it is highly probable the resort had closed by the time the Miles Company began construction. The abundance of menhaden provided a steady supply of oil and became a popular substitute for whale oil. It was also discovered that the by-products of these fish could be ground up and used as fertilizer for crops.

The Miles Company processed 8-15 million fish per year and the average yield was about 4-6 gallons of menhaden oil per thousand fish processed.[55] The company used twelve fishing vessels, and employed about forty men in the fishing end of the business and another twenty men in the factory work.[56] The factory itself was considered advanced in its design and was described in a government report[57] on fisheries:

> The factory of The George W. Miles Company at Milford, Conn., is said to have been the first one built after the model now universally followed, with cooking-tanks and oil-presses upon the second floor of the building. When the fishing fleet comes in, the fish are hoisted from the holds of the vessels into cars, in which they are carried over an inclined tram-way to the upper story of the factory building. Here they are turned into tanks, 20,000 fish in each, and cooked by steam-power. Then the water is drawn off and the cooked fish are placed in perforated iron curbs, which are so arranged upon railways that they can be pushed under a hydraulic press. Each curb-load of fish is subjected to a pressure of sixty or seventy tons, by which the greater part of the oil is extracted. The scrap is then dropped to the cellar below.

Not only did the Miles Company have a facility on Charles Island, they also maintained a self-sufficient factory-ship that did the same work as the island facility. The *Alabama* was constructed upon the hull of an old man-of-war and was primarily used in St. John's Bay, Maine.[58]

In 1873, local resident William B. Stoddard, brought a lawsuit in New Haven Superior Court[59] against the Miles Company and attempted to have the business cease its operations. Stoddard, himself a member of a law firm in New Haven, lived on the lower end of Gulf Street and was one of the town's residents who lived closest to Charles Island. Residents in town were outraged by the lawsuit and a petition was circulated by S. B. Gunn and signed by 123 others. They believed "the stoppage of said business on Charles Island would be a serious detriment to the interest of the town"[60] and requested a town meeting be called to take action.

William B. Stoddard's Home

Milford's Fish Oil and Guano Companies, 1868
Author's Collection

A town meeting was held on May 15th 1873 to discuss the town's options. About 300 (!) residents attended the meeting and it was voted, "That it is important for the interest of this town that the business of 'The George W. Miles Company' in manufacturing manures, oils, etc. from whitefish, as the same has been carried out at Charles Island should continue to be prosecuted without molestation." They also voted "That our representatives in the General Assembly be requested to endeavor to secure the repeal or modification of all statutes, under color of which, the reasonable prosecution of said business at that place may be hindered or interfered with."

The nature of the case is not revealed in existing Superior court records. It is likely that given the proximity of his residence to the factory, the unpleasant smells that exuded from the place might have been the focus of the dispute. Stoddard may have dropped the case or reached an out of court settlement, as it does not appear to have gone to trial.

Advertisement for Geo. W. Miles Co., 1871 [61]

About that time, Stoddard became a judge in the City Court of New Haven and maintained residence in that city during 1874 and 1875,[62] though keeping his Gulf Street property. Perhaps the intensity of the dispute diminished the farther away he lived from the fish works.

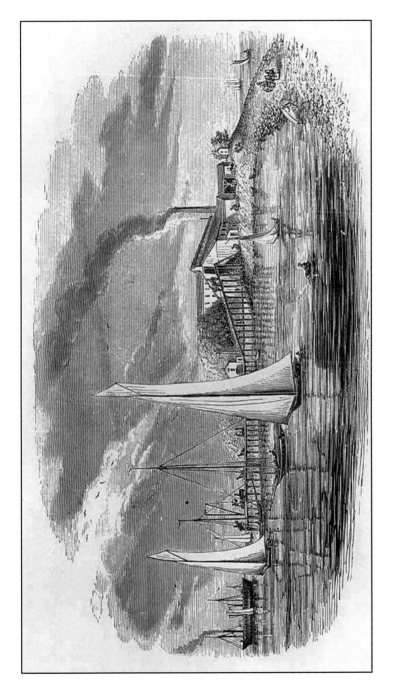

George W. Miles Company & Floating Factory Off-Shore, c. 1877
Freshwater and Marine Image Bank, University of Washington Libraries

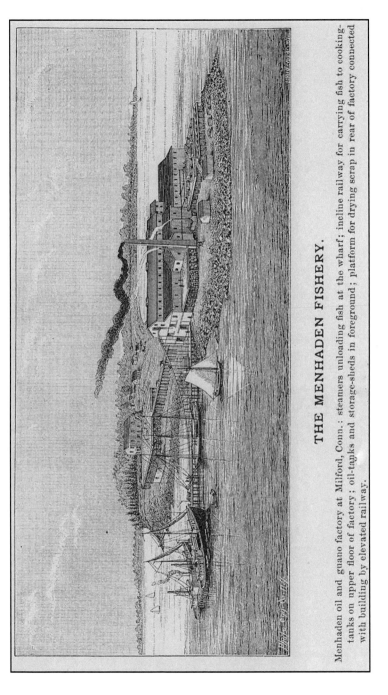

THE MENHADEN FISHERY.

Menhaden oil and guano factory at Milford, Conn.: steamers unloading fish at the wharf; incline railway for carrying fish to cooking-tanks on upper floor of factory; oil-tanks and storage-sheds in foreground; platform for drying scrap in rear of factory connected with building by elevated railway.

George W. Miles Company, c. 1885
Freshwater and Marine Image Bank, University of Washington Libraries

The George W. Miles Company thrived over the next ten years and won an international award at the Fisheries Exhibition in England in 1883. Their menhaden oil won a silver medal and then they took home a bronze for their fish guano.[63] As proud as the owners of the company must have been for their accomplishments, they were soon to face serious financial problems back home. In 1885, creditors of the Miles Company met in New Haven to investigate the financial standing of the company. Its assets were being overtaken by its liabilities and it appeared headed toward insolvency.[64] A trustee was appointed for the company but owners refused to surrender its assets.[65] Meanwhile, the town of Milford, which had rallied around the Miles Company in the Stoddard case, filed an injunction of their own. Apparently, the odors from the plant permeated the town and the waters surrounding the island had become contaminated. A bitter court dispute between the town of Milford and the Miles Company erupted and ended in May 1886[66] when the judge made permanent an injunction against the company, thereby shutting down its Charles Island operation.

The final closing of the fish oil plant may have been a relief for the island's owner, Sarah Prichard, and she had already begun searching for new tenants. After the resort hotel had closed, it quickly went into disrepair. Salt air winds blasted the paint away, unwelcome visitors broke its windows and "rooms were charred with the fires of the many clamroasts of vagrant picnic parties."[67] It sat unused and abused for some sixteen years and suddenly there was a glimmer of hope that it might be brought back to its former glory.

It had been rumored in several newspapers that the American Yacht Club was going to either purchase or lease a portion of the island[68] for a clubhouse and summer anchorage. The yacht club, founded in New York City by financier Jay Gould and other steam-yacht owners, was in fact searching for a waterside home and considered purchasing Charles Island. In the meeting minutes of the American Yacht Club[69] in 1884 there are two references to the island – the first in February mentions the title to Charles Island being "perfected." Since there was no change of ownership recorded in town records, it appears part of the island may have been leased by the club for part of that year. One yachting magazine[70] described the plans for the island:

> "A three story building, now standing on it, will be converted into a suitable club-house. It is proposed to make the island a summer recreation centre for the club, their friends and families. Several thousand dollars will be expended in improving the property, fitting up the club-house, laying out grounds for tennis and other out-door games, wharves, buoys, stationary anchors, etc. It is believed that many of the yachts will winter at Milford Harbor."

Jay Gould's 248' Yacht, *Atalanta*, c. 1880s
Courtesy of the American Yacht Club

Before these ambitious plans could be carried out, tragedy again struck the island. In the late evening of August 7, 1884 a fire of unknown origin started in the old, unoccupied hotel. Milford residents on shore at Burns' Point and Meadow's End witnessed the brilliant demise of the abandoned resort. It was reported the next morning:

> The flames were bursting out and soaring high up into the air, painting land and water with a sea of gold. It was the old Pritchard homestead, the large rambling structure on the

center of the island, which with its adjuncts is the only building that was ablaze. In an hour it was a mass of rosy cinders. The thrilling spectacle was witnessed by hundreds of sleepy summer boarders along the shore. Then the fire slowly died out, leaving the notable little island, one mile off the Milford shore, even more lonely than ever.[71]

The owners of the hotel had no insurance to cover the complete loss. The fire, combined with the George W. Miles Company insolvency, undoubtedly resulted in a financial setback for the heavily mortgaged Sarah Prichard and her investors.

The membership of the American Yacht Club changed its mind about the club's use of Charles Island. With the main building on the island now destroyed and the feeling among members that Charles Island was too far from New York City to make it a permanent home, they searched for a more convenient anchorage. The meeting minutes from September 1884 refer to "disposing of the interests" of the club at Charles Island. In 1887, they purchased property at Milton Point in Rye, New York for $6,000 and their new clubhouse was completed the following year. A devastating fire in 1951 destroyed most of the club's historic records and unfortunately no photographs survive from the brief Charles Island period. How different Charles Island would be today had the American Yacht Club bailed Sarah Prichard out of her debt and built their clubhouse on the island.

Charles Island went into foreclosure in 1888 and a woman named Elizabeth F. Noble of Brooklyn, New York took possession in June of that year. Noble's husband had died in 1865 and left her nearly $200,000. She was a shrewd investor and more than quadrupled her inheritance by the time she died in 1909. Mrs. Noble held the mortgage on the island for $7,247.50[72]. After a financial panic in 1893, she became fearful of becoming poor and losing everything, and started to live below her means. She moved to Mansfield, Massachusetts and purchased a small house, kept only one maid, did much of her own work around the property and even purchased cracked eggs because they were cheaper.[73] Perhaps to raise money to fight off her self-imposed poverty, she sold her island investment in 1902.

Aquinas Retreat House

Charles Island transferred ownership once again and the Connecticut Railway and Lighting Company purchased the island in 1904. At one point, CR&L wanted to build a trolley line from Milford to Charles Island.[74] The company planned to build an amusement park on the island to compete with Savin Rock in West Haven and passengers would be carried back and forth on tracks built over the sandbar. This plan was never implemented, perhaps due to the immense cost of the project, although CR&L maintained ownership of the property for nearly two dozen years.

As the United States moved closer to joining the war in Europe in 1917 the government began examining the coastal defenses along America's shores. The *New Haven Evening Register* reported[75] a lighthouse keeper believed he had sighted German U-Boats off Montauk Point at the outer reaches of Long Island, a report that later proved to be false. Nevertheless, caution ran high and the news account continued, "These waters are ideal for U-boat warfare, since the submersibles would find innumerable little coves about Montauk Point where they would harbor at night and even draw supplies from German agents on shore, meanwhile keeping close touch through spies with American shipping traffic." The federal government was concerned that German submarines were cruising the waters off the United States coastline preparing to make a "spectacular blow at American ports or shipping" once war was declared.

Another newspaper account stated that Charles Island had been identified as "a defensive point to help protect Bridgeport and vicinity from submarine attack."[76] Plans were said to be in the works to build a submarine-chaser base with a wireless station, searchlights and gun emplacements. A week after this plan was reported, the United States declared war on Germany; even so, the base was never built.

Path to the Retreat
Author's Collection

In 1927, the Dominican Fathers from St. Mary's parish on Hillhouse Avenue in New Haven announced they would build a layman's retreat center on Charles Island.[77] The effort was led by Father Edmund A. Baxter, a dynamic Dominican priest and former chaplain in World War I. During several summers, he and groups of teenage boys from the parish and other (mostly volunteer) workers cleared the land and built a small complex of wood frame structures. A chapel, dining and recreation hall, about fourteen cabins (each baptized with a different saint's name),[78] a grotto, walking paths, and Stations of the Cross were built and eventually it would accommodate up to fifty men. It was a simple retreat with few amenities. Yet, it was estimated that by the time it was completed, the cost of constructing the complex was about $100,000. Still to be built when the retreat opened was a heating plant that would allow winter retreats and a suitable dock to facilitate the arrival of "retreatants."

Original Chapel of Saint Thomas Aquinas
Author's Collection

59

View of the Cabins
Author's Collection

Shortly before the retreat opened, tragedy struck workmen from the island on Easter weekend in 1929. Late afternoon on Saturday March 30th five men and a teenage boy had been working at the retreat center to prepare it for its opening in the summer. They attempted to return to the mainland in a rowboat with a small outboard motor. Something happened, that only they knew, and the boat capsized about 1,000 yards east of Charles Island. Some of them clung to the overturned craft, but the cold water numbed them and one-by-one they let go of their last hope and slipped into the water, which was some sixty feet deep.

The dead from New Haven were William H. McDonald, age 63, a retired plumber; his son Burton McDonald, age 32, a plumber; Sabato DelFranco, age 52, a laborer and father of seven children; John J. Clerkin, a carpenter; and Walter Fallon, age 15, a junior at New Haven High School. The sixth drowning victim was John Oliver Balmer, age 47, the caretaker for the retreat center and a resident of Charles Island. He lived in one of the cottages with his wife; their son was studying to become a priest at a seminary in Ohio. The tragedy struck deep in St. Mary's parish and in the community at large. It was speculated the boat's load may have shifted, throwing the little craft off balance. The lack of an assignable cause was unsettling for everyone. The following Tuesday, the *New Haven Journal-Courier* printed an editorial that read in part:

The Charles Island Drownings

The Charles Island tragedy must sober and sadden the glibbest. How was it possible for six men to perish, within plain sight of land, in broad daylight, with very little sea running? ...Where such a tragedy has a ready explanation in some flaw of safety measures, some obvious fault or shortcoming in men or their devices, the gloom of it may be dissipated by rigorous efforts to mend the defect. But no such defect is visible in this terrible accident. The boat, apparently, was sound. Its motor, apparently, was good. Its crew, apparently, were competent. The sea, apparently, was not particularly menacing. There certainly is no special danger at the spot...There appears to be no criticism we may make which will alleviate the pain that six drownings give us. The occurrence merely makes us feel a little humbler...[79]

St. Christopher Shrine Dedicated to the Victims
Dominican Archives, Providence College

The facility opened a few months later and held its first retreat on the weekend of July 4th, 1929. Dominican priests held their annual retreats there, as did groups of male parishioners from the New England states, New York and New Jersey. Typical retreats for laymen lasted one weekend and were held from June to September. No honorarium was set by the Dominicans, relying instead on the generosity of the guests.

The Aquinas Retreat had been founded as a temporary refuge for men seeking "solitude and rest from the crash of worldly interests" and called it an "ideal location for a tranquilization of the soul." The island was beautifully maintained by the Fathers with many varieties of shrubbery and trees, particularly lilac bushes and cherry trees. The Dominicans described their tranquil setting, "This plateau of verdure, ringed about with rocks, nestles in charming peace and beauty in the blue waters of the Sound."[80]

The Grotto
Author's Collection

Solitude and rest were not the order of the day on August 4, 1930. On that day, the island was opened to the parishioners of St. Mary's in celebration of the Feast of Saint Dominic and six-hundred guests were accommodated. After Holy Mass was celebrated (with a fifty-voice choir) they were served lunch and had the run of the island to play ball, go swimming, and explore. One year later an estimated 1,500 visitors helped celebrate the Feast Day on Charles Island.

Boys from the New Haven and Milford area were hired to assist with maintenance of the property. They were poorly paid but were fed their meals and allowed to stay on the island if they chose. Those that lived at home and made the daily trip to the retreat house walked out at low tide and returned with the next low tide.[81]

By 1931, the wooden chapel that was originally on the grounds was replaced with a stone chapel constructed near the same spot. Several other additions were made to the retreat center during 1931 and were listed in the church bulletin.[82] New Statues of Our Lady, St. Dominic, and St. Christopher were received in July and placed in the grotto in St. Dominic Grove. The statue of St. Christopher was placed on a rock pedestal at the north end of the plaza and was erected to the memory of the men who lost their lives returning to the mainland on Holy Saturday, 1929.

Shrine of Our Lady
Dominican Archives, Providence College

A seventy-foot flag pole was erected under the supervision of Capt. B. L. Wright of Milford. The pole took the place of the signal that was on the high point at the center of the Island. It was used as a point of reference for the oyster-dredging boats to take their bearings. Also, the little retreat expanded its capacity. A dormitory building, having accommodations of eleven beds, was completed by the first of August. A Bell Tower was also erected that spring, built of stone gathered from the shore, and on it was placed the bell (weighing about 300 pounds) received from a Mr. E. E. Regan. The statue of Our Lady was mounted on a rock pedestal fronted by a stone altar on the path to the north of the Bell Tower.

The Bell Tower
Dominican Archives, Providence College

A Station of the Cross

Sacred Heart Shrine

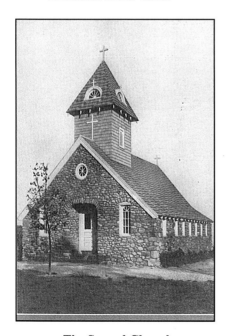

The Second Chapel

Cherry Lane at the Retreat

Dominican Archives, Providence College

66

The Aquinas Retreat was a popular destination for several years, though financially it wasn't very healthy. The Dominicans eventually closed the facility in the mid-1930s and moved off the island. When word of this event spread around the Milford community, it prompted some locals to pillage the island retreat bringing anything that could be carried or taken in a boat back to the mainland. They removed sheets, blankets, kitchenware, paintings, and any other items left behind that weren't nailed down. The island retreat center lay in disuse for a few years before the next willing buyer came along.

Scarce Pamphlet for the Aquinas Retreat
Author's Collection

Quadrangle with Second Chapel
Dominican Archives, Providence College

In 1938, the New Haven County High Sheriff, J. Edward Slavin, negotiated with the Dominicans to use their facility as a school/camp for the First Offenders Crime Prevention Club. Slavin was a visionary who believed in reform but didn't believe the traditional reformatory system offered youths a chance.[83] Slavin even wrote a script for a film along these lines that was produced in 1939. The film was *First Offenders* and had the tagline, "Stop turning kids without a chance into men without hope!"[84] The movie starred Walter Abel and Beverly Roberts. The goal of the Charles Island plan was to offer educational and recreational opportunities for boys between sixteen and twenty-one, who had a brush with the law, in order to help them stay out of trouble.

On the 19th of September 1938, the *New York Times* reported that Slavin had announced his intent to purchase Charles Island for his crime prevention effort. Yet, land transfer records show no change in ownership of the property at this time. It is highly probable that events two days later undermined the deal. On September 21st, the Great New England Hurricane of 1938 pummeled the Connecticut coast. With sustained winds of over 90mph and gusts up to 125mph combined with 14-18 foot tides, the retreat buildings on the island suffered devastating damage. Little remained of the complex after the storm and apparently Slavin's bid to purchase the island and its facilities was withdrawn. Slavin's progressive plan was eventually implemented, but not on Charles Island. In 1942, he and Daniel J. Adley established *Boys Village* in Milford. It still stands today, renamed *Boys and Girls Village*, at its original site on Wheeler's Farm Road.

The Dominicans eventually sold Charles Island in 1941 to Walter A. Peck of Westport and two years later the First National Bank & Trust Company acquired it in trust for another party. The identity of the actual owner was shrouded in mystery for the next six years. Curiosity and speculation was rampant as to who actually owned Charles Island. In March 1949, and after the *Milford News* conducted an investigation into the island's ownership, it was announced that United Illuminating Company was the actual owner. As World War II had approached, the company was asked by the federal government to add to their generating capacity. The company acquired Charles Island, as well as property between the shore and railroad tracks to the north to be used for transmission lines.

After the attack on Pearl Harbor, the government changed the focus from adding more plants to increasing the output at existing plants. The expansion of the facilities at its other power plants negated the immediate need for new construction on Charles Island. As time went on, there was some talk of a nuclear power plant being built on the island. In 1957, the President of United Illuminating addressed the Board of Directors on the issue, "the Company's property at Charles Island in Milford, Connecticut, may be a satisfactory location for a future atomic power station but a specific investigation must be undertaken to determine whether this particular location is practicable."[85] Fortunately, no power plants of any sort were built and the tranquility of the island the Dominicans had so cherished was preserved.

View of the Quadrangle & Paths
Dominican Archives, Providence College

Back to Nature

The State of Connecticut acquired Charles Island from United Illuminating in 1981 and it became part of Silver Sands State Park. In 1995, it was discovered by the Connecticut Bureau of Natural Resources that herons and egrets had begun to use Charles Island as a nesting colony. Four years later, Charles Island was declared a Natural Area Preserve to help protect the native bird population.

Young Black-Crowned Night Herons
Paul J. Fusco / CT DEP Wildlife Division

The island is now a breeding ground for the Black-Crowned Night Heron, Little Blue Heron, Great Egret, Snowy Egret, and the Glossy Ibis. Wildlife surveys are conducted every three years to determine the success of the rookery. In 2004, nearly 300 pairs of herons and egrets used the island's resources up from under 200 pairs in 1995. The biggest threat to the breeding of these magnificent birds is human disturbance, hence the closure of the island during the nesting season. Visitors should be aware the island is closed from May 24th through September 9th to protect the nesting areas.

There is another story that hasn't been completely told. Over the years, numerous boating and swimming accidents have occurred in the waters surrounding the island. Several dozen people have lost their lives within sight of Charles Island...some due to storms that capsized boats, others due to carelessness, inexperience, or bad luck. Many individuals have become stranded on the island forgetting to take the incoming tide into consideration. A strong current and surprisingly deep water make it almost impossible to return across the sandbar once it has begun to be covered. The beauty of the island and the solitude it offers its visitors are a strong attraction but be assured, the forces of nature are equally unforgiving.

The Lost Literature of Charles Island

Several published stories have made use of Charles Island either as a setting or as inspiration for their authors. In 2004, a children's book named *Kidd's Kids* was written by Kathleen Schurman. A treasure hunter named Oklahoma ("O.K.") Smith, attempts to locate Captain Kidd's treasure on the island using modern technology and is outwitted by six beach kids. The kids want to protect the legend of Charles Island and know that once the treasure has been found there will be no more "treasure island" to captivate them.

Kidd's Kids was not the first work to use Charles Island as a backdrop. Well over 100 years earlier Elizur Prichard's daughter Sarah J. Prichard (1830-1909), who had aspired to and succeeded in becoming an author, intertwined elements from her life on Charles Island into her written words. Sarah succeeded in publishing several books and dozens of articles in a variety of newspapers and magazines. She kept a handwritten list of her publications among her personal papers[86] but unfortunately kept copies of only a handful of the articles themselves.

Sarah J. Prichard
Collection of Mattatuck Museum
Waterbury, CT

Efforts to track down her writings in some obscure nineteenth century publications have met with considerable success and at least two of them have distinct ties to Charles Island. "My Pets on Ausantawae" and "A Trick of My Black Pink" were written for children and relate to the animals Sarah befriended when she spent her summers on the island. Sarah also wrote several books including *Martha's Hooks and Eyes* (1860), *Marjie's Matches* (1866), *Rose Marbury* (1871), *What Shawny Did to the Light*

House (1871), *Aunt Saidee's Cow* (1873), *Only Woman in Town and Other Tales of the American Revolution* (1898), and *Shawny Wade* (1909). She was also a major contributor to Joseph Anderson's *Town and City of Waterbury, Connecticut* (1896).

Sarah Prichard also wrote *The Wonderful Christmas in Pumpkin Delight Lane* (1908). On the 1835 map of Milford, "Pumpkin Delight" was the name of the area just northwest of what is now Silver Sands State Park. Pumpkin Delight Road and Pumpkin Delight School are the modern reminders of this old section of town. In this book, Prichard made several mentions of Charles Island (though not by name) and even described the fish factory activities in some length.

In 1868, Sarah wrote *Faye Mar of Storm-Cliff*. This Gothic romance with the Civil War in the background uses a large coastal mansion as the setting. Although Storm-Cliff wasn't located on an island, it stood perched on a steep cliff overlooking the ocean. At one point, Sarah described the sounds at Storm-Cliff and one cannot help but wonder how her words were influenced by having lived in that grand mansion on Charles Island.

> ...The low booming of ocean-surf always lingered about the region of Storm-Cliff. The thunders of the great deep shook the whole beach that night as the waves dashed the sand and rock ... Storm-Cliff, with its large lonely rooms, and its mid-winter quiet...[87]

Several decades later, American newspaper editor and author Irving Bacheller (1859 – 1950) wrote a story, "Lost in the Fog," that appeared in *St. Nicholas* magazine in 1901. A woman known as Mother Tipton and a young boy were sailing across Long Island Sound to sell geese when a dense fog rolled in and disoriented them. Mother Tipton's geese saved the pair and they were all stranded on Charles Island for the night.

Most of these stories haven't appeared in print since they were originally published and have been long forgotten. In order to preserve this aspect of Charles Island's history, three of these "lost" stories are reprinted herein for the first time in a very long time.

My Pets on Ausantawae

by

Sarah J. Prichard

The Evangelist, 1865

(Note: This article was part of a series that described Sarah's pets and the wildlife on Charles Island – describing the swallows, hens, cats and other animals that made their home on the island. These articles refer to Charles Island as *Ausantawae*, a variation of the name of the Indian Sachem and Prichard's resort Ansantawae House. It is uncertain if this spelling was intentional or an error by the publisher.)

Do you wonder what sort of a place Ausantawae can be? I will tell you all that history has whispered to me regarding Ausantawae; not this one, but the original individual who owned the name.

He was a very wise and powerful and old Indian, who is believed to have lived about ten or eleven score of years ago. Indeed he was so very grand in his Indian estate, that he was Sachem of all the tribes dwelling for more than a hundred miles along the great sea line, and higher into the uplands than I can tell you of.

Sachem Ausantawae owned, as his especial kingdom, a little territory surrounded by very blue salt water. It was scarcely more than a mile round about it; but there it was. Quite apart from the old mainland, and in the soft Summer days that came then, even as now, his true and loyal people arose from the forest afar and near and built Ausantawae a "big wigwam" on this tiny bit of an island. From that time to the end of his days the red chieftain summoned hither the warriors during the Summer.

He said in his mighty dialect, "Braves! Come to salt!" and obedient they came. They gathered clams from the sand on the beach and the mud on the shore, from under the rocks, and from the "bogs"; round-clams and long-clams, squaw-clams, and clams of every degree, and stringing them after the manner of apples, dried them in the sun for Winter use.

Think of a circle of young Indians, seated on rocks and the sand in the dusky twilight, threading clams! In silence they work until some maiden, duskier than the twilight, utters "Quahaug!" and immediately a young brave comprehending that she wants clams, that her work waits for them, supplies the article.

But Ausantawae was not one of my pets. He has departed. His wigwam no longer points toward the sky. Its very foundation man knoweth not. Ausantawae, his warriors, and the maidens of all the tribes, come not again to this bit of earth. The poor Indian! Who can tell where he lies buried?

When white men came here they gave to the place another name, with nothing the least bit attractive or nice about it. I like the old name, and often think of Sachem Ausantawae, and wonder if he liked and loved these rocks and shores, this green grass and blue of sea and sky, the breezes that sigh and gales that sweep as I like and love them; what kingly forest shade he sat under here, and where his council fires burned? Alas! I find not even the ashes from them. Nothing but a few whispers that have floated into old histories, tell of the earliest dweller here.

All this time my pets have been waiting to be "written about."

I said good morning to my king-fisher a few minutes ago, and she returned my salutation with so charming a bend of her stately head over the rampart of her airy castle, that for a moment I was subject to the temptation of giving you a fragment of the history of the quaint foreigners who are tarrying here for a while; but I was saved from unfaithfulness by the troop of stay-at-home hens that met and surrounded me. Just past the plum-tree I was taken prisoner, and naught could ransom me but fair kernels of yellow corn.

I do not think that hens have the slightest education concerning "weights and measures." I really think they believe themselves to be all wings and feathers. They fly to my shoulders or the top of my head if there is the slightest suspicion of corn about me. By the time I have one perched on either shoulder and two or three on the rim of my corn basket, I am ready to flee in at any open door that kindly waits to give me protection. My hens are so badly "brought up," that I retire to a second-story window and from thence drop the corn down for the society of seventy. I've taken a "census" since I've told you of the swallows,[88] and my report was correct.

Travelling (sic) is generally stated to be an improvement to the manners, but I do not think the hens on Ausantawae are the least mite of evidence that the statement is founded on fact; for they certainly are travelled (sic) hens. I cannot tell how many journeys they have taken by rail.

On the last occasion then they migrated in a large wooden box, the said box was waiting at a transfer station for the train, and I, the conscious owner of the box, was sitting a little apart with covert watchfulness over the familiar heads that peered up through the slats, as two men passed near. They were employed on the railroad.

"Ah! Hens!" said one.

"Why, don't you know them hens?" said the other, "they go up every Fall and down again every Spring.[89] I thought everybody knew them hens;" whereupon the two men drew near the box to make further acquaintance with my pets, and I stole away, not being exactly ashamed of the hens, but not anxious to claim ownership just then.

It is sixteen months since I made a journey of sixty miles to feed hens. They were three days missing, having been carried astray. Saturday afternoon came and no arrival of my cargo. Knowing that unless they fell into kindly hands starvation must be their portion, and armed with a basket of corn the search was commenced. Stowed away in the dark corner of a freight-car, in a just as dark freight-house, were the poor straylings. You can imagine the pet names I gave them; but the creatures paid little attention to me, it was all devoted to the Indian-corn or divided between it and the water given them.

Hens have a wonderful memory for locality. One Winter passed without the customary migration. Eighteen months surely is a long time for a hen to remember where she slept; but no sooner was the prison-house opened than out jumped "old Whity" and away she went for the barn. The door was closed, she looked up and down, tried the cracks of the door, but suddenly animated by another thought, she sped around the corner to the opposite side, where she doubtless remembered was another door. In a minute she was inside and had found her old roosting place, I do believe, on the same round of the ladder where she had passed many nights of Winter.

There she waited until a sense of loneliness and homesickness for her nightly companions and the perch on far-away Ausantawae came too strongly to be resisted. Down flew the hen and out where the strangers were wandering to and fro, entirely lost and utterly unable to locate for the night. She chattered away for awhile, going up quite close to one hen and another, then leading the way a few steps at a time, and going to and fro many times, until she induced four to follow her to the barn and the ladder. It was a week before the last one became convinced that the barn was a better covert than the blue sky from November winds. "Whity" was a very wise hen; well do we remember her, and the large white eggs she left in the nest. Some of the little children who knew Whity may read this. I am certain that they will not have forgotten her or her dainty, aristocratic, henly ways, nor how she went about for many months with five chickens, calling and feeding them when they were as large as their leader. Poor Whity! She died one day in the Spring of the year, of asthma, mourned by all the hens perhaps, certainly by all the family.

...I haven't told you the hundredth part about my hens, but I must pass them by, for there are the dogs and the cats, and the weasel and the cow, all the birds in the meadow and on the shore, the wild geese and ducks, and the glorious strangers that come and go, whose names I do not know, and last of all the American eagle, who has tarried here in the Autumn of the year ever since I can remember. If any one says, "I don't want to hear about them," I will be as quiet as a mouse.

A Trick of My Black Pink

by

Sarah J. Prichard

The Nursery, 1870

My Black Pink ran all over the garden; for he was a dog. Now, the garden where he ran was on a small island in the sea; and I will tell you what Pink did one morning.

I was sitting in the sun on the sand; and the sea was all blue and gold; and the baby waves were dancing up and down, as nothing but baby waves can dance. Up above my head, right in the grass, a tiny kitten was hiding; and down on the sand, by my feet, lay Pink. Oh, how black he was! -- not a bit of white about him anywhere. He kept his eyes on the grass where kittie was, a few minutes; then up he jumped, and ran right up the bank, and sprang into the grass. All in a minute the dog ran past me again, and in his big mouth *was the little kitten.*

"Pink, Pink! – you naughty dog!" I cried, "come here, this minute." But Pink did not mind me one bit. He just stopped half a second, or about that time, turned his eyes back at me, as if he would like to make them say, "I am only doing my duty, ma'am;" then he gave one solemn wag of his tail, and plunged off into the sea with kittie in his mouth.

I ran down close to the water, and called and begged and scolded; and my Black Pink paid no more attention to me than he did to the rocks on the shore.

Around and around the dog went. Once or twice he dropped the kitten a little way out from his mouth, just to see if it could swim. Then back he came to the shore, laid kittie, all wet and cold, on the sand, shook himself, gave kittie two or three hints with his paw to get up and shake herself; but kittie did not mind: so Pink rolled her over and over in the sand, until there was such a big bundle of sand that nobody would think there was a kitten inside it.

Collection of Mattatuck Museum, Waterbury, CT

Then he took up the bundle, and carried it up the bank and laid it in the sun, and stood a long time looking at it.

I picked up the kitten, and was carrying it to the house to rub off the sand and dry the poor thing; and, as I was on the walk, I met John the gardener, and told him what Pink had done. "Oh! it won't kill the cat," he said. *"Pink gives it a bath every day; and kittie likes it when she gets dry."*

I am afraid some one will think this a made-up story, if I do not tell you that it is true; that I saw it; and that it happened on a little island in Long-Island Sound, where I have spent many summers, and about which I could tell you stories enough to fill "The Nursery" a whole year.

S. J. P.

Lost in the Fog
by

Irving Bacheller

St. Nicholas: an Illustrated Magazine for Young Folks, 1901

It's odd how some people take to geese. As a boy I never could understand, for the life of me, how one could ever have any love of a goose in him. When I came out in the glory of my first trousers a whole flock of geese came after me, tweaking the sacred garment with their bills, and hissing me to shame of my new dignity, and screaming in derision as they pulled me down. After that and for long I treasured a most unrighteous hatred of the whole goose family. They were to me a low, waddling tribe with the evil spirit of envy in them.

The worst thing about Mother Tipton was her geese, I used to think. She lived in a shanty all by herself, – a lonely man-hater, – and the bit of land that climbed to the ridges on either side of it was known as Mother Tipton's Hollow. Every day skirmishers, sentinels, and reserves of geese covered the green slopes of the Hollow, and a white squadron of them was always sailing the black waters of the pond in its center. I came betimes, of a summer day, and peered over the circling ridge in a tremble of fear, whereupon a stir of white wings and a yell of defiance greeted me. Mother Tipton herself was a kindly creature who rescued me whenever I was captured by that noisy rabble of boy-haters. She was an Englishwoman, the daughter of a rich man, I believe, in the city of Bristol, and turned out of her home for some reason – we never knew why. I know she had in her shanty wonderful trinkets of gold and silver, the relics of a better day, and more than once I had the inestimable pleasure of holding them in my hands. The Hollow was half a mile from the shore of the broad Sound, and Mother Tipton took her geese and feathers to market in a rowboat. There was a big town across the bay, and she went always from the end of Shirley Point when the weather was fine, rowing as strong an oar as any man of all the many that made their living on those waters.

One morning – I was then a boy of eight years – I got permission to go with her in the boat. I remember she had a cargo of ten young geese, that were stowed away, their legs tied together, in the bow of the boat.

It was a mile and a half across the bay, and the water lay like a mill-pond, with scarcely a ripple showing. A thin mist hovered about the farther shore as we pulled away, but we could see the dock clearly and the building that lay beyond it.

"Land o' Goshen!" Mother Tipton cried, after rowing a few minutes, "it's a foggin';" then she sat a long time, as it seemed to me, looking over the water at a misty wall that lay not far ahead of us. Of a sudden she began to pull vigorously on the right oar.

"It's the ebb-tide," said she, "and we must get back as quick as we can or we'll be in trouble."

Evidently she saw it coming, for she began to pull with redoubled energy. I could just see the dim outline of rocks on Shirley Point as we turned about.

"The tide has taken us half over," she muttered. "It runs like a mill-race."

Now I could see mist rising on the water under the side, as if it had turned hot suddenly. The fog thickened fast, and presently the boat had seemed to lengthen, and we to go far apart, so that I could see but dimly the face of Mother Tipton. Then I could hear her groan and breathe heavily as she put all her strength to the oars. She was lifting the bow from the water every stroke now, but suddenly I heard the snap of an oar, and the boat turned in the tide; then a splash of water hit my face.

Mother Tipton rose in the boat and shouted a long halloo. We listened for some answer, but, hearing none, she called "Help!" a dozen times, at the top of her voice. Between her cries we could hear nothing but the tide rippling under the boat.

I felt a fine thrill then, having little sense at best, and none of the danger. I remember growing very manly and chivalrous when I saw Mother Tipton crying in her seat, and did my best to comfort her.

She was up shouting for help again presently, but not a sound came back to us. We drifted, of course, with the tide, and could see nothing. She kept calling all the time, and when my tongue was dry for the need of water, and the thought of cake and cookies kept crowding on me, I lost a bit of my bravery. It was time to be getting home – there was no longer any doubt of that.

"Mother Tipton," I said, "where do you suppose we are?"

"The Lord only knows, child," was her answer. "I'm afraid we're out in the deep water half over to Long Island. But the tide has turned, and it may take us back before night comes. We'll just sit still and keep calling."

I was lying on my back in the stern, resting my head on the seat behind me, and was feeling very miserable indeed, when I heard a great disturbance among the geese.

"Willie, come here," said Mother Tipton. Two of the geese were lying in her lap, and she unwinding a long fish-line.

"Tie it tightly," said she, "just above the big joint of the leg. Wait – let's cut it first into even lengths. That's right – now cut it."

She measured for me, and I cut the line, as she held it, into ten pieces, with probably as many feet in each. Then we tied them securely to the geese, above the big joint of the legs, and fastened the loose ends together, winding them with a bit of string. We tied another fish-line to this ten-stranded cable, cut the geese apart, and let them all go at once. They flew for a little distance, and, being not all of a mind, came down in a rather bad tangle. I had hold of the line, and if I had not paid it out quickly we would surely have lost them. They ducked their heads in the water, and shook their wings, and screamed as if delighted with their liberty.

Meanwhile they had begun to pull like a team of horses, and I could feel the stretch of the line. It had parted in a minute, – and a thick, strong line it was at that, – and I had gone overboard and was clutching for the loose end. There was a thunder of wings when they saw me coming upon them, and when I got my hand on the cord they began to pull me through the water at a great rate. I was a good swimmer, but was glad to lie over on my back and rest a little after the violence of my exertion. Then, suddenly, I heard the voice of Mother Tipton calling me, and it seemed far away. I looked in the direction it came from, and then I got a scare I hope never to have again. I could see nothing of the boat. The geese were swimming with the tide, and, over all, the fog lay on the sea as thick as darkness. I was breathing hard, and lay for a long time floating on my back, my fingers clutching the tight strings.

When I turned over and got a little of the water out of my ears, I could hear faintly in the distance the voice of Mother Tipton calling the geese just as I had heard her many a time over there in the Hollow. I could see them turn and listen, and then the whole flock veered about, cackling together as if they knew the meaning of it. The ten of them were now swimming comfortably. Every moment I could hear more distinctly the voice of Mother Tipton, and after a little I could hear the water on the boat. Suddenly its end broke through the wall of fog, and I saw my companion looming above me in the thick air, her head showing first. She answered with a cheery "Thank Heaven!" as I called to her, and the whole flock rose out of the water and tried to fly.

The geese came up to the boat-side, and she touched their beaks fondly with her hand as she came to help me in. The water had chilled me through, and I was glad enough to set my feet on the boat-bottom, and to take off my coat and wrap my shoulders in the warm shawl that Mother Tipton offered. You may be sure I kept a good hold of the strings, and before I sat down we made them fast to some ten feet of the small anchor-rope and tied it at the bow. Then those that had got their feet over the traces were carefully attended to. They lay quietly under the gunwale as Mother Tipton fussed with them, sometimes lifting one above another. She shooed them off in a moment, and they made away, turning their heads knowingly as she began to paddle.

"I believe those creatures will have sense enough to go ashore. They know more than we do about a many good things," said she. "That old gray gander of mine goes a mile away sometimes, but he'll get home, if it *is* foggy, every night of his life."

Mother Tipton's Geese
Courtesy of the Yale University Library

It was growing dark, and in five minutes we couldn't see our team. I was kneeling in the bow, my hand on the rope, peering to get a view of the geese, when I heard a loud quacking and a big ripple in the water just ahead. I was about to speak, when I saw a drift of dark objects on either side of the boat. I made out what they were, and caught one of them by the neck just as Mother Tipton shouted, "Ducks!" Then there was a roar of wings that made me jump back, and that set the geese in a panic. I hung on to my captive, and brought him in flapping and drenching my sleeve with spray.

"Bring him here," said Mother Tipton, as I crept to the middle seat, the poor creature fighting me desperately all the way.

"We shall need him for our supper, my dear child," said she, as she took him. "I think we're coming to shore somewhere, and I know you're hungry."

It was not long before we heard our boat-bottom grinding on the sand, but it was very dark. Mother Tipton went to the bow of the boat, and I was near the middle seat.

"Thank Heaven, we're somewhere!" I heard her say; and then she stood up, and I heard her paddle strike in the sand, and felt the boat lift forward and go up on the dry beach. I was out pulling in a moment, and I tell you the firm earth had never so good a feeling. I felt my way up the beach, and Mother Tipton came after me. It was so dark and foggy we could see nothing. After a little I felt the grass under me, and my companion lit a match and touched it to a bit of paper she had taken off of a bundle in the boat.

"Make haste, now," she said, "and pick up all the bits of small wood you see around."

The dry drift lay all around us, and in half a minute a good bit of it was crackling on that flaming wad of paper. Then we brought sticks as thick as a man's leg, and fed the flames until they leaped higher than our heads and lit the misty reaches of the shore a good distance.

"Lawsy me!" said she, presently, "I think we're on Charles Island." Then she took a brand out of the fire, and walked away in the thick grass waving it above her head. She was calling me in a moment.

"Bring the fish-line and the tin pail!" she shouted.

I went to the boat for them, and was shortly groping through the tall grass in the direction of that flickering torch. She was not nearly so far away as I thought, the fog had such a trick of deepening the perspective in every scene. I found her by an old ruin of a house, peering into a deep well, the cover of which had mostly rotted away. We were not long tying that line to the pail and dropping it down the well-hole. The line raced through my fingers, and the pail bounded as it struck, and rang like a bell on the splashing water. When I had hauled it up, we sat looking at the slopping cylinder of cold, clear water, the golden flare of the torch shining in it, each insisting that the other must drink first, until I was quite out of patience.

She took the pail at last, and buried her mouth at the rim, and nearly smothered herself with the water. I thanked her with a good heart when I got my hands on it, for I had a mighty fever of thirst in me. When my dry tongue was soaking in the sweet, pure water, I could feel my heart lighten, and soon it was floating off its rock of despair.

"Now let's take a pailful with us, and get supper," said Mother Tipton. "We're on Charles Island, five miles from home, but it isn't more than half a mile from Milford. We'd better stop here for the night, and maybe it'll be clear before morning."

I took the torch, and she dragged behind her a bit of the fallen roof that had once covered the old house. By the light of the fire we began to dig clams with the oar and paddle. In ten minutes we had enough for a fine bake, and laid them out on a rock, and raked the hot coals over them. Mother Tipton had killed and dressed the duck, and while I tended the clams she was cutting turf and shaking the clay off it into a hollow she scooped out of the sand. She wet the clay then with salt water, and, when it was thick and sticky, rolled the duck in it until the bare skin was coated. Then she poked it into the ashes under the hot fire, and came to help me uncover the clams. We ate them with sharpened sticks, and, while some butter would have helped a bit, they went with a fine relish. The duck came out of the fire looking like a boulder of gray granite. Mother Tipton broke the hard clay with a stone, and the duck came out clean and smoking hot, leaving its skin in the shell. A more tender and delicious bit of fowl I have never eaten, the salt clay having given it the right savor.

After supper we untied the flock and set it free, and dragged the boat above tide-water. Then we drove two stakes in front of a rock near the fire, and set our strip of roofing over all. Under it we threw a good layer of hot sand from near the fire, and built high ridges on either side of our shelter. There were sacks of down for pillows, and my overcoat and the big woolen shawl as covering. Though it is so long ago, - I was, as I said, only eight years old, - I remember still when Mother Tipton told me to creep in and draw up the wraps around me. The warm sand gave me a grateful sense of comfort. I lay for a time and looked at the dying firelight, but before long I fell asleep.

As I woke, next day, I could hear the bellow of a great fog-siren, away in the distance, that sent its echoes crashing through the dungeon of mist. Next I noticed the sound of the noisy water on the rocks near by. It was growing light, and somebody was poking the fire. When I lifted my head I felt a warm breeze and saw that the fog had gone. A man with a wooden leg and a patch of gray whiskers on his chin was standing by the fire. I crept out and greeted him, rubbing my eyes with drowsiness.

"Ketched in the fog, I suppose," said he, kicking the fire.

"Yes, sir," I answered; "we were caught by the tide and lost, yesterday."

"Hum!" he muttered, as he glanced under the lean-to roof of our shanty and took a good look at Mother Tipton. "Rather a tidy bit of a woman – stout as an ox an' a good-looker."

"I'd thank you not to disturb her," I said with indignation.

"Not for the world," he answered, returning and shying another bit of wood at the fire. "I like t' see 'em sleep – it's good for 'em. Got anything for breakfus'?"

"I'm going to dig some clams," I answered.

"You jes' wait," he said, winking at me, "an I'll go off to the tug an' bring ye some coffee an' fish an' bread an' butter. Got loads of it aboard there. No trouble at all."

He made off for his boat, that lay on the beach near by, and rowed around the point. I walked down the shore a few rods, and from a high rock saw the tug lying at anchor a little way off the shore. He came back in a short time, bringing a basket of provisions. Mother Tipton was up, and by that time I had a good fire going.

"Madam," he said, laying down the basket, "may I be so bold as to offer you su'thin' for your breakfus'? Here's a snack o' coffee an' fish an' a tidy bit o' bread an' butter."

She thanked him politely, and while we were getting breakfast, he told us that he was menhaden-fisherman "- as owned his own tug." Then we told him our story. Afterward he insisted on taking us home. We were glad to accept his kindness, and the sun was shining brightly when we put off for the tug, with all our geese in the boat; I made Mother Tipton promise me that not one of them would ever be sold. The captain brought a big armchair and made her very comfortable in the bow of the boat. We were home in an hour, and I was as glad to get there as all were to see me. The adventure resulted in great good, for it gave me some respect for geese, and gave Mother Tipton a greater regard for men. It was not long after that she added to her museum in the Hollow a man with a wooden leg; and you may be sure I went to the wedding.

Sunrise over Charles Island
Paul J. Fusco

References

Abbot, Henry L. *Beginnings of Modern Submarine Warfare Under Captain Lieutenant David Bushnell*. Willetts Point, NY: Battalion Press, 1881.

Abbott, Susan Woodruff. *Families of Early Milford, Connecticut*. Baltimore: Genealogical Publishing Company, 1979.

"American Prize Ring," *National Police Gazette*, 25 June 1881.

American Yacht Club Meeting Minutes, 1884.

Anderson, Joseph (editor). *The Town and City of Waterbury, Connecticut*. New Haven: Price & Lee Company, 1896.

Andrews, Wayne (ed.). *Concise Dictionary of American History*. New York: Charles Scribner's Sons, 1962.

Aquinas Retreat On Charles Island. New Haven: Dominican Fathers, (1929).

Bacheller, Irving. "Lost in the Fog," *St. Nicholas Magazine*, February 1901.

Barber, John Warner. *Connecticut Historical Collections*. New Haven: John W. Barber, 1836.

Beers, F. W. *Atlas of New Haven County*. New York: F. W. Beers, 1868.

Benton, Joel. *A Unique Story of a Marvellous Career: The Life of Phineas T. Barnum*. Edgewood Publishing Co., 1891.

Boston Daily Globe.

Bryant, William Cullen and Sydney Howard Gay. *A Popular History of the United States*. New York: Charles Scribner's Sons, 1888.

Bushnell, David. David Bushnell Papers, 1783-1956. Yale University Archives and Manuscripts.

(Butler, William Allen.) "Nothing to Wear: An Episode of City Life," *Harper's Weekly*, 7 February 1857.

Collections of the New York Historical Society (2nd Series, Vol. I). New York: 1841.

"Connecticut Justice," *New York Evangelist*, 21 April 1870.

Day Book of Adolphus Baldwin, Milford, Connecticut, 1833-1841. Located in the Connecticut State Library.

Dow, George Francis. *The Pirates of the New England Coast 1630-1730*. Salem: Marine Research Society, 1923.

Downes, William Howe. "An Old Connecticut Town," *The New England Magazine*, November 1889 (New Series, Volume 7, #3), 268-281.

Fassett, John D. *UI: History of an Electric Company*. United Illuminating, 1990.

Frank Leslie's Illustrated Newspaper, 30 April 1870.

Gardiner, Curtiss C. *Lion Gardiner and His Descendants, 1599 - 1890.* St. Louis: A. Whipple, 1890.

Goode, George Brown. *The Fisheries and Fishery Industries of the United States.* Washington: GPO, 1887.

Hannah, Archibald. *A Brief History of the Thimble Islands.* Branford: Archon, 1970.

Hartford Daily Courant.

Historical Sketches of the Town of Milford. New Haven: Tuttle, Morehouse and Taylor, 1914.

History of Milford 1639 - 1939. Federal Writers' Project: Milford Tercentenary Committee, 1939.

History of Milford 1639 - 1939. Federal Writers' Project Original Research Notes, Correspondence and Draft Copies located in the Connecticut State Library.

Hoadley, Charles J. *The Public Records of the Colony of Connecticut (1706 to 1716).* Hartford: Case, Lockwood and Barnhard, 1870.

Howe, Henry F. *Prologue to New England.* New York: Farrar & Rinehart, 1943.

Internet Movie Database, 2006. http://www.imdb.com.

Jameson, J. Franklin. *Narratives of New Netherland 1609-1664.* New York: Charles Scribner's Sons, 1909.

Janvier, Thomas A. "The Sea-Robbers of New York." *Harper's New Monthly Magazine.* November 1894.

Lambert, Edward R. *History of the Colony of New Haven.* New Haven: Hitchock & Stafford, 1838.

Lewis, Tom. *The Hudson: A History.* New Haven: Yale University Press, 2005.

Middlebrook, Louis F. *Maritime Connecticut During the Revolution 1775 - 1783.* Salem: The Essex Institute, 1925.

Milford Citizen.

Milford Connecticut 325th Anniversary 1639-1964. Milford, 1964.

Milford News.

Milford Directory 1913. New Haven: Price & Lee, 1913.

Milford Property Transfer Records.

Milford Town Meeting Minutes.

Neal, Daniel. *The History of New England.* London: J. Clark, 1720.

New Haven Daily Morning Journal-Courier.

New Haven Directory. New Haven: J. H. Benham, 1872.

New Haven Evening Register.

New Haven Journal-Courier.

New Haven Sunday Register.

New Haven Superior Court Docket, May 1873.

New York Times.

Obituary Record of Graduates of Yale College. New Haven: Yale University, 1870-1900.

Papers of John Cotton Smith, Collections of the Connecticut Historical Society, Volume 4. Hartford: Connecticut Historical Society, 1954.

Prichard Collection 1747-1920. Mattatuck Museum, Waterbury, Connecticut.

Prichard, Sarah J. "A Trick of My Black Pink," *The Nursery*, February 1870.

Prichard, Sarah J. *Faye Mar of Storm-Cliff.* New York: Wynkoop & Sherwood, 1868.

Prichard, Sarah J. "My Pets on Ausantawae," *The Evangelist*, 29 June 1865.

Proquest Historical Newspaper Databases.

Report of the Commissioner - United States Commission of Fish and Fisheries. Washington: GPO, 1879.

Saint Mary's Church Monthly Calendar. New Haven: April 1929, January 1931, March 1931, November 1931.

Sand in Our Shoes. Milford: Walnut Beach-Myrtle Beach Historical Association, 2004.

Saturday Chronicle, 15 September 1906.

Schurman, Kathleen M. *Kidd's Kids.* AuthorHouse, 2004.

Snow, Edward Rowe. *True Tales of Buried Treasure.* New York: Dodd Mead & Company, 1952.

Steinke, Thomas J. *Proposal to Rebuild Penfield Reef as a Dredge Spoil Peninsula for the Purpose of Stabilizing the Fairfield, Connecticut Shoreline.* February 28, 1982.

Stowe, Nathan. *Sixty Years' Recollections of Milford.* Milford, 1917.

Townshend, Charles Hervey. "The Early History of Long Island Sound and Its Approaches." *Papers of the New Haven Colony Historical Society*, Volume V. New Haven: Printed for the Society, 1894.

"Valley of the Naugatuck," *The National Magazine*, November 1857.

Waterbury American.

Wilcoxson, William H. *History of Stratford.* Stratford: Tercentenary Commission, 1939.

Wilson, James Grant and John Fiske. *Appleton's Cyclopedia of American Biography.* New York: D. Appleton and Company, 1888.

"Yachting," *Outing and the Wheelman*, April 1884.

Zacks, Richard. *The Pirate Hunter: The True Story of Captain Kidd.* New York: Hyperion Books, 2002.

Notes

[1] A "league" is an old unit of measuring distance at sea. It has become standardized as 3.18 nautical miles (6,080 feet in a nautical mile). The measurement has varied from country to country and over time.

[2] Johan De Laet's account is found in Jameson, *Narratives of New Netherland 1609-1664*, 44.

[3] *Collections of the New York Historical Society* (Second Series, Volume I), 296.

[4] Townshend, "The Early History of Long Island Sound and Its Approaches," 291.

[5] *Collections of the New York Historical Society* (Second Series, Volume I), 307.

[6] Lambert, *History of the Colony of New Haven*, 85.

[7] Lambert, *History of the Colony of New Haven*, 85.

[8] Barber, *Connecticut Historical Collections*, 240.

[9] Abbott, *Families of Early Milford, Connecticut*, 219.

[10] Hoadley, *The Public Records of the Colony of Connecticut,* volume V, 214.

[11] Dow, *The Pirates of the New England Coast*, 75.

[12] Wilson, *Appleton's Cyclopedia of American Biography,* volume III, 531.

[13] Zacks, *The Pirate Hunter*, 382-383.

[14] Bryant, *A Popular History of the United States*, volume III, 35.

[15] Lambert, *History of the Colony of New Haven*, 147.

[16] Downes, "An Old Connecticut Town," 276.

[17] This was probably Thomas Welch (son of Thomas and Hannah) baptized in 1658. He married Elizabeth Peck and died in 1707.

[18] This was probably Zachariah Whitman who married Sarah Fitch in 1702 or 1703. His birth date is not known but he likely died in 1752.

[19] Various records refer to Kidd as "Robert" including his original commission from the King of England to hunt pirates.

[20] This may be Thankful (Strong) Baldwin, born in 1663 and married to Jonathan Baldwin c. 1695 after the death of his first wife in 1693.

[21] Lambert, *History of the Colony of New Haven*, 148.

[22] Hanna, *A Brief History of the Thimble Islands*, 82.

[23] Gardiner, *Lion Gardiner and His Descendants*, 100-101.

[24] "No Kidding: Island Holds Gold, Treasure Hunter Insists," *New Haven Register,* 15 September 1992, 1.

[25] Lambert, *History of the Colony of New Haven*, 133.

[26] Lambert, *History of the Colony of New Haven*, 135.

[27] Ezra Lee to General David Humphries, 20 February 1815, David Bushnell Papers.

[28] *Papers of John Cotton Smith, Connecticut Historical Society Collections*, 114.

[29] Milford Property Transfer Records, Volume 32, 213 (September 14, 1835).

[30] "Its Last Misfortune," *New Haven Evening Register*, 8 August 1884, 4.

[31] Day Book of Adolphus Baldwin, 1833-1841.

[32] "Its Last Misfortune," *New Haven Evening Register*, 8 August 1884, 4.

[33] "Items." *Hartford Daily Courant*, 17 July 1855, 2.

[34] Prichard Collection, Mattatuck Museum.

[35] "Summer Resort," *Hartford Daily Courant*, 13 May 1858, 2.

[36] "Charles Island," *Waterbury American*, 24 July 1857, 2.

[37] Classified Ad. *Hartford Daily Courant*, 1 July 1857, 3.

[38] "The Valley of the Naugatuck," *The National Magazine*, 385.

[39] Butler, "Nothing to Wear," *Harpers Weekly*, 84.

[40] Editorial, *Hartford Daily Courant*, 19 August 1858, 2.

[41] "Fire on Charles Island," *Hartford Daily Current*, 2 August 1859, 2.

[42] Classified Ad. *Hartford Daily Current*, 28 May 1866, 2.

[43] "Locals Convention," *Hartford Daily Courant*, 2 August 1866, 8.

[44] "Its Last Misfortune," *New Haven Evening Register*, 8 August 1884, 4.

[45] State Matters, *Hartford Daily Current*, 4 May 1866, 2.

[46] Advertisement, *Hartford Daily Courant*, 30 July 1866, 8.

[47] Advertisement, *Hartford Daily Courant*, 10 July 1866, 7.

[48] "Miscellaneous," *Hartford Daily Courant*, 10 August 1866, 1.

[49] Benton, *Unique Story of a Marvellous Career*, 609.

[50] *New Haven Directory 1872*, 63-64. This description appears to have been reprinted from an earlier publication without having been updated. All indications are the resort had closed by 1868.

[51] Unless otherwise noted, all quotes relating to the prize fight are from "The End of Prize-Fighting in Connecticut" & "The Milford Raid," *New Haven Daily Morning Journal Courier*, 13-14 April 1870.

[52] "American Prize Ring," *National Police Gazette*, 25 June 1881, 10.

[53] "Won on a Foul," *Boston Daily Globe*, 30 April 1891, 4.

[54] "Connecticut Justice," *New York Evangelist*, 21 April 1870, 1.

[55] *Report of the Commissioner - United States Commission of Fish and Fisheries*, 86-89.

[56] *Report of the Commissioner...*, 189.

[57] Goode, *The Fisheries and Fishery Industries of the United States*, 344.

[58] *Report of the Commissioner...*,165-168.

[59] New Haven Superior Court Docket #696, May 1873.

[60] All quotes in this section relating to this meeting are from the Milford Town Meeting Minutes, May 15, 1873.

[61] Advertisement, *Hartford Daily Courant*, 19 April 1871, 4.

[62] *Saturday Chronicle*, 15 September 1906, 10.

[63] "The Fisheries Exhibition," *Hartford Daily Courant*, 29 October 1883, 3.

[64] "Additional State News," *Hartford Daily Courant*, 14 May 1885, 3.

[65] "News of the State," *Hartford Daily Courant*, 1 January 1886, 4.

[66] "News of the State," *Hartford Daily Courant*, 8 May 1886, 4.

[67] "Its Last Misfortune," *New Haven Evening Register*, 8 August 1884, 4.

[68] "News of the State," *Hartford Daily Courant*, 9 August 1884, 4.

[69] American Yacht Club Meeting Minutes, February & September 1884.

[70] "Yachting," *Outing and the Wheelman*, April 1884, 78.

[71] "Its Last Misfortune," *New Haven Evening Register*, 8 August 1884, 4.

[72] Milford Property Transfer Records, Volume 55, 321-322 (June 22, 1888).

[73] "Mrs. E. F. Noble's Will Attacked," *Boston Daily Globe*, 16 November 1909, 9.

[74] "Filed with the Secretary," *Hartford Courant*, 1 January 1903, 3.

[75] "U-Boats Believed Near," *New Haven Evening Register*, 30 March 1917, 1.

[76] "To Fortify Charles Island," *Hartford Courant*, 31 March 1917, 15.

[77] "To Be Dominican Retreat," *New York Times*, 26 September 1927, 20.

[78] *Sand in Our Shoes*, 500.

[79] "The Charles Island Drownings," *New Haven Journal-Courier*, 2 April 1929, 10.

[80] *Aquinas Retreat on Charles Island*, 13.

[81] *Sand in Our Shoes*, 500.

[82] *Saint Mary's Church Monthly Bulletin*, November 1931.

[83] "Sheriff Turns Island to Crime Prevention," *New York Times*, 19 September 1938, 21.

[84] Internet Movie Database, http://www.imdb.com/title/tt0031312.

[85] Fassett, *UI: History of an Electric Company*, 361.

[86] Prichard Collection, Mattatuck Museum.

[87] Prichard, *Faye Mar of Storm-Cliff*, 8 & 223.

[88] This refers to an earlier story in this series about swallows that lived above the verandas at their Charles Island house.

[89] Apparently, the Prichard family transported their chickens by rail to and from Waterbury when they spent an extended period on Charles Island.